Sandman
Blues

Sandman Blues

Stéphane Bourguignon

Translated by David Homel

a novel

Published in French in 1993 by Editions Quebec/Amérique

Published in 1996 by
Stoddart Publishing Co. Limited
34 Lesmill Road
Toronto, Canada
M3B 2T6
Tel. (416) 445-3333
Fax (416) 445-5967

Canadian Cataloguing in Publication data is available from the National Library.

ISBN: 0-7737-5783-X

Cover Design: Bill Douglas /The Bang
Computer Graphics: Mary Bowness
Text Design: Tannice Goddard
Printed and bound in Canada

Stoddart Publishing gratefully acknowledges the support of the Canada Council, the Ontario Ministry of Citizenship, Culture and Recreation, Ontario Arts Council, and Ontario Publishing Centre in the development of writing and publishing in Canada.

For Thérèse and for the little beast who was born that year

My appreciation to François Avard for his continuing interest and Dominique Blanc for the objectivity

PART 1

1

It was true, since Florence left, I hadn't really done much — the bare minimum had been good enough for me. But now, I swear, all that was over with; it was completely in the past. Tonight had been an exception. It had nothing to do with her, I just wanted a few hours to myself, a fistful of minutes, a tiny grain of sand from the great hourglass of eternity. I wasn't asking for much.

Rosemary's Baby was playing on TV, and I had enough beers in the fridge to gently propel me into the arms of Morpheus. But I hadn't even popped my first top when Pierrot showed up in my room, carrying on about how eight months was enough, and how he couldn't stand seeing my hangdog look anymore, and that the time had come to get my ass in gear.

I grumbled into the bathroom, cut my two-hundred-and-forty-day beard, and slipped on a clean T-shirt. He was downstairs on the sidewalk waiting for me. I didn't bother asking where we were going. I just put my ass in gear.

•••

"I'll get us some beers," he announced, sliding off his stool.

"Might as well." I cast a world-weary look around the place, getting a fix on how humanity had progressed during my period of lethargy.

It looked as though I hadn't missed much. People were still wearing pastel colours and they had their hair spiked into submission with gel. There was a perfect example, a redhead of the male species bouncing up and down on the dance floor. A piece of heavy machinery programmed to disgust. Especially girls, it looked to me. Needless to say, he wasn't paying attention to the ugly ones. But that girl over there had a superb body, and she moved it with such sensitivity that you could see pure music issuing from every pore. The whole construction was trembling like the heart of a lioness when the gazelle quivers under her cruel paws. She was a message from the gods telling us there were still a few worthwhile things on this planet.

Unfortunately, the guy stuck to her like glue. Put a grass skirt on him, jab a bone through his nose, and *voilà,* you'd have a famished cannibal prancing around a pot.

Pierrot came back with two beers. He put them on the little table behind us.

"There's a two-for-one on imports."

One swallow told me why. They export the stuff because nobody drinks it in the country where it's brewed.

"Nobody's here," he told me. "I looked around, just in case, but no dice."

Nothing shocking there, since Bill and Paule are our only friends. Bill likes places where the music won't let you talk, so he can cogitate at his ease, but Paule doesn't like it when Bill cogitates, so they've stopped coming here since they started going out together. To console Pierrot, I pointed out the big carrot-top; I know he likes to savour the spectacle of human stupidity.

"How long has he been hanging around her?"

"Two or three minutes."

His dance, which was already pretty borderline, had degenerated into the DTs. He whipped his body fore and aft, shook from top to bottom, and every time the drummer's stick hit the cymbals, it was like lightning had struck his butt. I wondered whether he was going to stop of his own volition, or whether we'd have to perform an exorcism.

"Is that girl on her own?"

"Sure, Pierrot . . . like all of us."

"That guy's starting to bug me."

Pierrot's mind might be as twisted as a pretzel, but his soul is noble and upright. He's the kind of guy who would rob a bank and help a little old lady cross the street on his way to the getaway car.

The girl walked off the dance floor. It was a matter of survival. Carrot-Top hadn't laid a hand on her. He'd just done a rain dance around her, a little psychological harassment, just to keep in shape.

She moved in my direction, eyes dark and jaw set. I got the feeling that she knew I hadn't been able to keep my eyes off her, and that I'd soon be paying for the sins of all those miserable creatures on earth who've got something hanging between their legs. She sat sidesaddle on a stool immediately to my left. Her beer was already there, which eliminated a whole set of hypotheses.

The big retard came up hot on her trail. Nice and easy, Pierrot and I turned ninety degrees on our chairs.

"You're a hell of a dancer," he launched in, wiping his forehead with his sleeve. "You must have taken classes, too."

Maybe, but I'd be willing to bet they weren't from the same teacher.

"Listen, I came here for a little peace and quiet. Thanks for the compliment, but I'd like to be alone."

"Maybe I can help you if something's not right," he said, rolling his big, brown, sensitive doe-eyes.

"Everything's just fine."

If she'd taken out a chain saw and started slicing up that pig, I wouldn't have minded getting splattered by the blood.

"Why don't you get a little fresh air with me? It'll do you good. We can talk about what's bothering you."

"You're right, something is bothering me. Something big and red that won't get off my case."

In a stew, some mouthfuls are harder to swallow than others. As he tried to cook up a witty repartee, Carrot-Top grabbed the girl's beer and drank down a mouthful. Pierrot had seen enough. He got up and walked over to the guy.

"I know it's none of my business, but I think the message is loud and clear. The girl wants to be alone."

"Hey, man, am I getting in between you and your boyfriend?"

I admit it, I was a little worried about how Pierrot would react. You might know someone like the back of your hand, but that doesn't mean he won't surprise you now and again. Between you and me, that's what gives love its sting.

Pierrot grabbed Carrot-Top's head and gave him a big juicy kiss, right on the ear. The guy slipped free, stared at Pierrot like he was the devil, and slunk off, rubbing the offended organ. Pierrot turned and came back to his chair, as if nothing had happened. Let me tell you one thing: it's great to have a hero as a friend.

The girl put her hand on my shoulder and aimed her dark eyes at mine.

"That was nice of your friend, but I could have taken care of it myself."

Let's get one thing straight. Pierrot and I aren't in search of glory; we prefer the silence of the hurricane's eye, the quiet trenches during the ceasefire, the ease of summer evenings on the verandah. That sums us up. I had to tell the girl that what we did was totally selfish. Thank you very much, now go in peace.

"Of course," she said, "I wouldn't have used force right away, but it could have come to that."

Of course, of course, we can all end up there. All of us could kill if the moment was right. The hard part, on the other hand, is being patient.

"My name's Sonia," she announced, knocking her bottle against mine.

"Oh, yeah, right . . . I'm Julien, and that's Pierrot."

She leaned over in my direction to take Pierrot's hand. Just far enough for a little cloud of perfume to work its magic under my nose. Something lighter than air, discreet as a spring deep in the woods. A few months ago, before Florence, I would have fallen like a leaf, but now I can smell a trap a mile away.

"Listen," Pierrot told her honestly, "don't feel you have

to talk to us just because of that. We didn't have anything in mind, you know, no ulterior motives."

"I know. I just feel like talking to somebody. I don't know a single person in town."

She wasn't trying to be mean, but let's face it, it wasn't the most complimentary thing to say either. Anyway, it didn't really matter to us.

"How long have you been here?" Pierrot asked.

Well, I guess it mattered a little bit after all.

"Three weeks. Are you guys from here?"

"Yeah, not too far. A half hour away, maybe."

"Really? I live right next door."

We were quiet for a few seconds, but only because we had nothing to say. You can't expect too much from accidental meetings. Actually, you can't expect too much from life in general.

The girl got up and disappeared into the crowd. For a second or two, we wondered what she was up to, then we stopped wondering about anything at all.

The disk jockey, on the other hand, knew exactly what he was doing. The dancers were literally eating out of his hand. For the last few minutes, he'd kept the level down, giving them a chance to catch their breath, but now he came back twice as loud with what must have been the latest hit. The little dance floor filled up in a hurry, and it was shaking so hard out there it looked like a school of herring swimming circles in a barrel full of brine.

Sonia came back, arms full of beer. I'd seen that label somewhere before.

"It was two for one, I couldn't resist. Go ahead, serve yourselves."

We couldn't really refuse — we bent ourselves out of shape showing how we could be nice, too. And that's how we discovered, over some miserable import, that she had come to town to try to find her place in the sun as a fashion designer. Ambition is a fascinating thing. It starts out subtly, and the further it goes, the bigger it gets. The pleasure you get when you reach your goal is the strongest thing going; it gives you the feeling that you really exist. Unfortunately, you can't get free of it, you kill yourself getting another hit of the feeling and end up dropping dead from the effort. Suicide becomes a form of asserting your existence. For the time being, Sonia wasn't asserting very much, since she was just a sewing machine operator in a garment factory. That made us comfortable enough to tell her that we lived off the government.

• • •

I was starting to get fed up. There's nothing more boring than watching assholes strut around, trying to excite the desired sex. I say "desired" instead of "opposite" because, these days, "opposite" excludes too many people. And what about the music? What did they do to the music? With the material that's been coming on the market the last few years, they could put on twenty different tunes and you'd swear they'd been playing the same one for the last hour.

We went outside. No regrets. Though you'd have to be crazy to leave a girl like Sonia alone. As soon as we turned away from her, a few sharks came swimming up, mouths open.

The cool April air swallowed us up like oysters. I breathed in a few good lungfuls to get my brain oxygenated. Which was going to come in handy, because Carrot-Top and two of his friends were waiting for us a few metres away. I looked at Pierrot. He was removing his fists from his pocket.

"What do you know? It's our two faggy friends!"

The biggest of the three didn't look like a star in the intelligence department, and the laugh he let out confirmed my impression. At times like these, I regretted having lost my religion: a god can come in handy sometimes. Okay, most of the time it's a pain in the ass, but still, you should be able to count on him once or twice a year.

"So it's back to the house for a hot time, huh, you fairies?"

I glanced behind to see whether we could retreat. Too late — a fourth guy had taken up position in front of the door to the bar. Luckily everyone was empty-handed. With weapons, there's not too much sport to it.

The air was electric, and the hairs on our arms stood up. Knowing Pierrot, the world must have looked to him like a series of black-and-red flashes. Mostly red, I'd say. I was the only one who wasn't surprised when he leaped at Carrot-Top's face.

Both of them hit the ground and Pierrot tried to stave in the guy's skull by using the sidewalk. Unfortunately, just as little red stains were beginning to appear, the big guy with the moronic laugh messed up Pierrot's fun by grabbing him around the middle. I just stood there, as stiff as aspic, as the third guy moved in on my miserable little person.

As my feet left the ground, out of the corner of my eye I saw Carrot-Top sink his fist into Pierrot's stomach. The next thing I knew, I was sitting on the ground with the left side of my face flooded by an incredible rush of heat. I wanted to touch it and see if I still had any skin left, but the guy was getting ready to get me to my feet again. Fortunately, a completely unreal scream froze everyone in their tracks.

The guy guarding the door suddenly collapsed at Sonia's feet. Her legs were slightly spread, her knees were bent just enough to hold up a locomotive and her hands were outstretched, ready to split a log in half. I used the diversion to slam my right foot into my aggressor's chin. The blow stood him up and since I'd put an extra helping of mustard on it, the guy fell backwards. Sonia stepped past me, jumped over the guy who'd just hit the pavement, and took hold of what I figured was a nerve in the neck of the big guy who was holding down Pierrot. The poor bastard tensed up a little, made not a sound, attempted not a movement, but his prisoner freed himself effortlessly. When Sonia let go, the guy slid to the ground like a lump of butter at room temperature.

Now that he was free, Pierrot jumped on Carrot-Top with his eyes bugging out and a vicious smile on his lips. The guy did his best to protect his face, but Pierrot knocked him down and used all his energy to send his nose around to the back of his head. Not that I didn't appreciate the show, but I figured it was time to intervene. Pierrot didn't want to let go, but with a little distance, he realized that Carrot-Top had gotten his money's worth. The poor guy was still flailing around with his arms and legs. At first I thought it was a nervous reaction, but then I saw it was his way of keeping the blood flowing.

"Come on," Sonia told us, "let's go to my place."

Might as well — the police were going to show up any minute. Not that we were guilty of anything, but we'd gotten kicked around enough for one day. We limped off at top speed towards Sonia's apartment. I wasn't particularly proud, but in a funny way, I was utterly happy.

As we stepped into her place, the red flashing lights were splashing the living room windows. Pierrot was in pretty bad shape, and we'd had to help him for the last fifty metres or so. He was having trouble breathing. We laid him on the sofa.

"Don't move," Sonia ordered, going off towards the bathroom. "I'll get something for your eye."

"What's wrong with my eye?"

"Nothing special," I said. "Just the colour."

Sonia came back with a little pot covered with Oriental writing. She sat down next to Pierrot and applied a liberal layer of cream over half his face.

"You'll see, that's the best thing for it. You can trust me."

That's for sure, I thought. Sonia is the kind of girl you're better off taking seriously.

The bathroom was jammed in between the kitchen and the living room. I pushed open the door and felt around for the switch, long enough to recognize that damned perfume, that scent as cool as the night. It was so good I practically lost consciousness. A woman's bathroom is a rose growing on a garbage heap. All those vials everywhere, those perfumes mingling together, those morning energies that never quite fade away . . . My God, it's enough to make you want to love one.

My upper lip was split a little, and there was dried blood around my mouth and under my left nostril. I hosed down my face with a few litres of icy water, hoping to give my blood the courage to circulate again. In my ears I kept hearing Sonia's scream of fury as she neutralized the guy by the door. It wasn't a human cry; there was something supernatural about it. She'd come to us from heaven, like manna. On the other hand, she could have showed up five seconds earlier and saved me from that fist to the face, but who can complain?

"You want something to drink?" she asked. "I've got Scotch, beer, and wine."

I moved into Scotch, always welcome after a few beers. Pierrot voted for red wine and Sonia for a glass of water. We sat on the sofa and sipped our little pleasures, describing the scene from every possible way imaginable: from Carrot-Top's point of view, from Sonia's point of view, from the sidewalk's. Slowly, but surely, our drinks went down and every milligram of alcohol moved through our bodies like a little cloud of opium.

"You should sleep here," Sonia said. "This is no time to go out on the street again."

"No, no, we'll go home, it's no big deal."

"No. You can take my room, there's a double bed there. I'll sleep here on the sofa."

"We're not going to throw you out of your bed. Julien will sleep on the sofa and I'll take the floor."

"Do you have to get up at any particular time?"

We answered in the negative. We didn't have to think twice or waste a fraction of a second asking ourselves that question.

"Perfect."

She escorted us to her room, took a sheet and blanket from the chest of drawers, and left us to ourselves. "Be good, you two."

I watched the door close behind her. Pierrot was already lying on top of the blankets. I turned off the bedside light and undressed, counting each stab of pain I felt in my legs and cheek.

My eyes riveted to the ceiling like a pair of steamed mussels gazing at the Milky Way. I listened to Sonia go back and forth between the living room and the bathroom. The alarm clock showed three fifteen, and the pillow was filled with the good scent of a woman.

"Good night."

Pierrot didn't answer. He was already in paradise.

2

The sheet was all twisted around my legs, and I didn't know how it happened — maybe I'd had a washing-machine dream. Pierrot was lying on his back, mouth wide open, both hands on his penis. Either he was dreaming about Sonia or about wrestling a dwarf. The swelling had almost entirely subsided — around his eye, that is. That made sense. A girl like Sonia would just naturally have a cream that was utterly efficient.

I rolled over on my left side. The alarm clock read ten minutes after noon. It was Friday, but we weren't late. Our unemployment insurance cheque wasn't due till next week.

I opened the door as slowly as I could. To be perfectly honest, I wouldn't have turned down the chance to watch Sonia sleep. That's how you learn about girls. Take the toughest ones, the real pains in the ass, the most pretentious ones — the only way to discover their weaknesses is while they sleep. The one before last who wrecked my life was like that. I would watch her sleep with her little clenched fists and her little frown and I couldn't believe it. That girl made the entire planet's life miserable when she was awake, but when she finally let go and relaxed a little, you could tell she was even afraid of sleeping. I felt like killing her a hundred times a day, but when I had the misfortune of seeing her drift off, tears would practically roll down my cheeks. That's how impressive the sight was. When it got too much to hold back, I'd wake her up and we'd have sex, then, peacefully, she'd drift back to sleep. That kept us together for a while, but when my insomnia gave out, we split up. Shit, Sophie, if only you could have slept your life away . . .

Sonia was wearing a kind of white kimono, and was destroying hordes of imaginary foes. A fist thrown here, an elbow chop there: she was like a Swiss watch. You could see the air split asunder, and if she repeated the same move a few minutes later, you could be sure she'd travel through the same tunnel she'd carved out earlier. Even the sun pressed its face against the window to watch the show as Sonia chopped up its rays into hundreds of innocuous little laser beams.

"Hi," I said.

She didn't flinch. Silence on her lips, marble in her eyes. Contained, controlled force, paid out in small doses like a plume of steam from a geyser. It gave her gigantic proportions. Sonia was like Samson slowly bringing down the columns of Dagon's temple.

I kneeled down by the wall. An Oriental beatitude settled over me, and I was suddenly terribly hungry for a number two dinner with double spare ribs.

She finished her routine on her knees, forehead touching the floor. In that light, she looked like an angel on a cloud, with an eye cast earthwards to watch over her protégé. Then she got to her feet, took a deep breath, and when she exhaled, a scent of ylang-ylang filled the room.

"Did you sleep well?" she inquired, giving her wings a little shake.

"Not bad."

Then she came so close to me I was sure she wanted to kiss me, so I offered my lips. She stuck her hand on my face, put her head close to my mouth, and inspected the insignificant wound I had at its edge.

"It looks fine."

"Thank you."

The conversation ended on that note, and we inhabited the perfect silence of the apartment while, outside, people ran and jostled one another, growling and barking. We sat there long enough to consider the space that contained us, and to anchor ourselves solidly enough to the ground to confront another day.

"Pierrot's still sleeping?"

"Like a baby."

Her hand closed over mine and she led me into the kitchen on tiptoes. I had no idea what she had in mind. You had to be ready for anything when you were with a creature from above. When it came to anticipating Sonia's next move, it looked like the cards were stacked against me.

The sight of the coffeepot reassured me. She filled two tall ceramic cups and put them on the table, between the sugar bowl and the carton of cream. Real cream! Some girls carry a little bit of paradise hidden up their sleeves.

The holy ambrosia flowed through our veins, and a few sparks began to glimmer in my dark brain. Sonia put away the dishes that were stacked in the rack, washed last night's glasses, wiped down the counters, stopping at the table from time to time to take a sip from the mug. I watched her discreetly, enchanted at having earned a place in the morning ritual of a new woman.

I couldn't help comparing her to the other girls I'd known. Florence was someone special, but Sophie — really! She would have made a beautiful corpse, but as far as living beings were concerned, she wasn't much. When I made the mistake of going out with her, if other guys showed her the slightest interest, she would raise her voice a notch and start laughing too loud. She figured her ass was worth its weight in gold. All right, she was beautiful. And her ass really was something special. I could spend hours watching it glow like the moon in the night sky. Perfection incarnate. When we broke up, she told me I didn't appreciate her for her true worth. Naturally, I didn't bother telling her that I used to spend all night contemplating her backside; that would have only soured her attitude. To end our affair on a high note, she used one of our dates to find herself a more appreciative guy. After a few hours of laughing and bellowing like a deaf woman, she let me know it was over by walking out on the arm of Mr. Appreciation. Thanks a lot, so long. I watched that ass go out the door and prepared a good wad of spit that I'm still keeping in the back corner of my mouth for her burial day.

We heard a whimpering noise. It must have been Pierrot sitting up in bed. We looked towards the living room and a few seconds later he appeared in the doorway. He looked like a woman who'd forgotten to take off her mascara before going to bed. Out of pity, Sonia offered him a chair. I poured him a cup of steaming coffee. The way to a man's heart is through his stomach.

"Aren't you working today?" he managed, raising two black holes in Sonia's direction.

"I called in sick. If you have nothing special on, maybe we could hang out together."

I gave a half-smile and waited for the excuse that Pierrot would concoct.

"We don't have anything else on."

"We could go for a walk," she said, "you know . . . look in the store windows or something."

"Window-shopping! Yeah, that'd be cool."

I didn't know why Pierrot was so enthusiastic. He'd never cared about shopping in his whole damn life. The only time he was willing to go into a store was to shoplift some clothes for us. As for our little fashion designer, she must have been bored stiff. First she had to save our lives, then take us back to her place, and, next day, while away the hours with us. Face the facts: there was nothing special about us. We were like an opening at an art gallery. You check out the pictures in a hurry, and afterwards, you have to drink a litre of wine if you want to be half social.

Pierrot and I hit the showers. Together, because, according to Sonia, there wouldn't be any hot water for the next two days otherwise. I closed the curtain while Pierrot worked the faucets. The water was ice cold at first, but I didn't care. He was under the showerhead, not me. He soaped up his hair and ears. When Pierrot sees bubbles, something goes *ding dong* in his brain and the whole mechanism goes crazy. He started shooting foam balls at me. My eyes and mouth were his favourite targets. We traded the soap, spelled each other off under the hot stream, and all that water flowing over our skulls and that feeling of freshness resuscitated us and gave us the strength to take the next curve at two hundred kilometres an hour.

When we came out, squeaky clean, Sonia was busy building a giant cheese omelette. Things were going smoothly: we had just met and our cruising speed was clicking already. I didn't know how long we could go on this way, but for the time being, the wind was favourable and all the sails wanted to do was snap in it. We did our bit for breakfast, and as soon as it was done, we threw ourselves like wild beasts on the poor, defenceless, newborn chicks. It was completely edible, the coffeepot was bottomless, and we were with a new-found friend — I figured happiness couldn't be far off.

"Would you mind if I showed you some of my drawings?"

"Not at all," Pierrot answered. "We'd love to see them."

She jumped up and ran to her room. Meanwhile, we filled our mouths to the brim, chewed a few seconds, then displayed the results to each other. Okay, maybe we didn't produce masterpieces, but it came from the heart and besides, the way the art market is these days, you could spit on a sheet of white paper and sell it to a museum for a million-six.

Sonia had enough material to cover every wall in the kitchen. I don't know anything about art, but I do recognize talent when I see it.

"You're that good, and you're still working in a factory?"

"I guess so," she sighed.

Pierrot can't stand injustice. He's not the kind of guy who'd let a talented girl like Sonia waste her time in a shitty job.

"When you think of all the assholes making it big — they don't even deserve to wash out the toilets with their hair."

And with those words, we all sank into sadness. We ruminated on how crummy society was and all kinds of other black considerations. Good thing there was that drop of cognac in the last cup of coffee to shake off the intimations of death that filled our heads.

•••

I had a green garbage bag crammed full over one shoulder. Pierrot was carrying a similar burden. Sonia? She was as free and energetic as a butterfly in heat.

"Don't give up, we're almost there."

Now I understood why she wanted to spend the day with us. She never would have been able to carry all this stuff on her own.

There were washers and dryers and a counter for folding clothes in the middle, and a machine instead of a little old lady for making change. We emptied the two bags onto the floor to separate whites and colours. Sonia climbed onto the counter to oversee our work. A pair of jeans on this side, a shirt on that side, an undershirt, oops, a pair of panties, ouch, another pair of panties. Lord, bless this day! A pretty girl's pair of panties is like the Host — it's how you take communion with the other world. Fifty years from now, when people will have to stop at every corner to breathe purified air dispensed by a vending machine, a pair of panties will still be my lifeline. Instead of dying with burned-out lungs, I'll pass away with circles under my eyes.

Just before he put the coins in, Pierrot took off his shirt and threw it into the machine with the colours. I decided to do the same with my T-shirt. Pierrot upped the ante by tossing his jeans in. I had no choice; I had to follow suit. Sonia was smiling. She was wondering whether we were going to stop there. Modesty is like Velcro: when you really get going, it's easy to pull it off. We stared each other in the eye, stock still like a pair of cowboys on a dusty main street. The first one to drop his undies wins the other's respect. Pierrot won, of course, and I had to pay him the tribute of my boundless admiration.

But we couldn't really walk around naked like the day we were born for the next thirty minutes, so we made ourselves a handsome green skirt out of the plastic bags. It wasn't the first time we'd done that, and it wasn't the first time Sonia had naked men around her either. But for the woman busy fogging up the window outside, it must have been a first.

The more time we spent together, the better we got along. Especially Sonia and Pierrot. There were all kinds of hints, everything from a smile to a touch to a look. Nothing too serious if you took each element on its own, but when they were all lined up together, the details started adding up. Like letters, actually. By themselves, they're meaningless pictograms with no personality. But once they're strung together with their brothers and sisters, they take on significance. Pierrot and Sonia were like letters: all they wanted was to make a word. It had to do with chemistry. You know, that certain imaginary something that snakes its way through the ether and rules our lives without asking our permission. Pierrot's waves met Sonia's wavelets, and let me tell you, there was a fine copulation in the small invisible world they made.

The rest of the afternoon we went window-shopping and received a complete explanation of the faults and qualities of such-and-such a design, and the weaknesses of such-and-such a material. I tried to give maximum space to Pierrot and Sonia. You have to know how to read between destiny's lines. One of love's great powers is to be able to separate two of the world's best friends. You can't stop it, it's sacred. Deep down, I was happy for him because it'd been a dog's age since he'd fallen for a girl. I was happy for Sonia, too, because she deserved the best this world had to offer. Actually, I was the only one I wasn't happy for.

"I think I'll go home now."

Pierrot looked at Sonia, then at me, then at Sonia again.

"I suppose I ought to go, too," he said, biting his lip.

All that's very nice, Pierrot, but what you two should do is spend the evening alone together, and afterwards hold each other all night and drink beer and smoke cigarettes. Besides, tomorrow is Saturday, and that way you can draw it out.

"No, you go ahead and stay. I've got things to do tomorrow, anyway."

"What's there to do?"

There was absolutely nothing to do tomorrow, but I was hoping the fool would catch on to my strategy. Sonia tried to look disinterested, except her right foot kept trying to dig a hole in the sidewalk.

"Oh, of course!" Pierrot exclaimed a little too obviously.

"It's true, I completely forgot. Sure you don't need me to help?"

"No, I'll be okay."

"Well, then, I guess I can stay. Unless Sonia's got other stuff to do."

"I don't," she told him. "I'd like it if we spent the evening together."

Sure, some things are more fun when two people do them together, but I wasn't really thinking that far ahead . . .

A friendly slap on Pierrot's shoulder and a kiss on Sonia's cheek, thanking her for everything. We began to move our separate ways, and after a dozen steps or so, I turned around to see what kind of couple they made. Pierrot turned around at exactly the same time, a big, foolish grin on his face.

3

The damn rain had been falling ever since I got up. A fabulous spring, weeks and weeks of beautiful sunshine, record warmth, and record sales for swimming pools and air conditioners, and on the day I have nothing to do, it has to rain pitchforks. I decided on a boiling hot bath, a giant-size mug of coffee, and a Michel Jonasz tape.

I tickled the drop hanging from the faucet with my big toe. I'd put the telephone next to the bathtub, the front door was unlocked, and my mind got ready to go wandering with its knapsack on its back. When my body is soaking in water, nothing can get me out. The bailiff can come and seize the furniture and I wouldn't lift a finger.

It must have been around one o'clock. I looked at the soap and thought of Pierrot. Normally, the morning after he meets a girl, he's back early. He likes to get up while the girl is still sleeping. After all, as he says, it's not her fault if

I feel like having sex with every woman I see at night, but can't stand the sight of a single one of them the next morning. Today, he was way past his usual time.

Michel Jonasz launched into his big hit. Shivers ran down my spine. The electric guitar shot through my brain. How could anyone resist? You can't, you picture your ex-girlfriends parading before your eyes, one after the other. Fortunately, Sophie's butt lingered on to reconcile me with life. It was worth the pain of birth, if only to watch that wonder of the world redefine modern geometry. The problem was that I couldn't stick with that image. I climbed the ladder of time frenetically like a salmon that won't stop until it returns to its birthplace. What could I do? Flo's the one who brought me into this world.

Florence and I had a care-giving relationship: she waitressed in a bar and I was half alcoholic. I used to hang out there every night to mumble a few words at her as I ordered my beer. I put away my share. Too bad about her boss — he wasn't easy, he watched her like a hawk. A kind of hyper-tense Chihuahua who barked over everything and nothing. The guy wasn't too honest either, always involved in some kind of deal.

One night, he told us to wait until after hours to get acquainted. We took him at his word and kept our traps shut, but right after closing time we went and fucked in the coat-check. Flo waitressed from six in the evening to three in the morning and I worked at a gas station from seven in the morning to four in the afternoon. When we came together, we had better things to do than talk about the weather. It would grab hold of us and with just one look, we knew it was going to happen. We wallowed in madness

— it had to take place in the next five minutes or else. Obsessively, we sought out somewhere, anywhere, hand in hand, looking everywhere, half-tortured by the thought that we wouldn't find it, half-blessed by the happiness of knowing what would happen once we pressed our bodies together. When we went to it, it didn't last more than a couple of minutes. We climbed the stairway of pleasure four steps at a time. We welded our mouths together, our hands immediately went rummaging in each other's pants. We fucked like crazy, spitting on heaven and the trouble it rained down on us. We stuffed the whole shit-bag of humanity into the oven and basted it with a piping-hot cup of lust.

Naturally, we didn't know what was in store for us. When you spit into the wind, you've got to figure that sooner or later something's going to land in your face. It landed last August. I left her at the bar and never saw her again. The gunman aimed at the Chihuahua, the bullet shot off his ear, but that wasn't enough. It had to end up in the middle of Florence's body.

My fingertips were as wrinkled as prunes. I stepped out of the tub and dried my face and hair, just enough to get the excess off because I like to run my hand through it and feel the moisture. Then came my arms, shoulders, and chest. The flannel towel shivered at the touch of a dozen majestically virile hairs.

I moved on to my back, and that's when that day's particular troubles began for real. I didn't know how I did it, but the towel ended up floating face-down in the bathtub. I wrung it out, redefining the concept of blasphemy.

The Jonasz tape finished and silence covered the apartment. That's when I heard the front door close.

"Pierrot!" I called out. "Do you want me to run you a bath? Or did you guys already take a shower?"

I waited for his answer, an ear-to-ear grin on my face and my shoulders shaking with laughter. After a few sterile seconds, I served up the same question.

"Pierrot? Do you want me to run you a bath, or did you guys already do it in the shower?"

A kind of vague uneasiness came over me.

"Pierrot?"

I decided to lock the bathroom door.

"*Pierrot!!*"

The doorknob rattled violently, and as I prayed to heaven that the lock would pass the test, a shoulder shook the whole structure of the door. I stood completely motionless, naked in the middle of the room, sweating blood and vinegar. My eyes travelled over the room as my frozen brain desperately sought some hard-hitting object. The footsteps moved towards the kitchen. I decided to breathe.

"*Pierrot, stop that!*"

The silverware drawer squeaked. I shivered. If that wasn't Pierrot, then the guy was getting ready to do a little butchering. The best defence is a good offence. I grabbed the lid at the back of the toilet, slid the bolt across, and slowly opened the door. As close to the wall as a fly is after it's been hit by a newspaper, I crept towards the kitchen. The shadow of a human being lay across the floor. It had a knife in one hand and something I couldn't identify in the other.

I don't know where the courage came from, but I leaped into the room with the enamel cover in one hand, ready to give as good as I got.

The guy was standing at the counter. In his left hand was an enormous knife; in his right, a peanut butter sandwich.

"Why didn't you answer?"

"Were you speaking to me?"

"Ha, ha, very funny. I can't stop laughing. I'm laughing so hard I think I'm going to pass out."

"Man, I just spent the most beautiful night in my life. I never thought I could be happy like that."

I almost stopped wanting to splatter his stupid brains between the wall and my cover. I lowered my weapon.

"I'm happy for you."

He took the first bite of his sandwich. It smacked around in his mouth for a few seconds.

"Sonia is absolutely incredible," he chewed. "She's the best thing that's happened to me in a hell of a long time. It's like everything is possible when I'm with her."

Obviously, Pierrot had been washed away by a wave of passion. He was looking at me, but I could tell he was still lost in Sonia's eyes. His feet had stopped touching the ground. There I was, half-listening to him, naked, with a toilet lid in one hand. We had about as much in common as a master plastic surgeon and a boxer.

"I think we're going to see each other again. That's the way it looks, anyway. It was hard saying good-bye, we couldn't imagine the next few hours without each other. I'm telling you, man, Sonia is some woman."

"Well, I'm happy for you."

"I think she's really going to be somebody in my life."

I put the lid down by the sink and my rear end on a chair.

"I swear, man," Pierrot went on, "what I felt with other

girls was nothing, it was like a firecracker compared to TNT. I mean, Sonia is a nuclear bomb."

"I'm happy for you."

I might as well face the facts. We'd been living together for two years now — it was time we moved on to something else; it was time to take the plunge. I wasn't going to start blubbering about it. Good for him if he found the girl he never saw in me.

"I suppose you fucked all night."

"No. We didn't even touch each other. We looked into each other's eyes, we told our life stories from A to Z, we laughed like crazy, then we fell asleep, just like that."

I knew it was over. We were sailing straight towards the coral reef, we were going to sink, we wouldn't even have time for a last breath before we went down, we were going to sink like stones. A good fuck can leave you blind for a few weeks, but when two people hit it off that well before they even lay hands on each other, there's nothing left to do but light a candle.

"I'm happy for you . . . When are you moving in with her?"

"Cut the crap, no one's moving anywhere. We only just met. Look, I don't know where all this is going to lead, but I will tell you one thing I don't think I've ever said before: if I'm going to settle down one day, she's the one I want to do it with."

A bead of water, a pearl of cold sweat, ran down the middle of my back.

"Go ahead, man, settle down with her. It won't make any difference to me."

It was stupid, it was melodramatic, but I couldn't help

myself. Life was pulling the strings anyway. Life sits back in the cheap seats and watches as you try to come to terms with the crummy little character you have to play, whereas you'd much rather have a walk-on part. Right now, for example, I'd be a hundred times happier in the role of the toaster instead of playing the role of this naked guy watching his only friend prepare to leave the scene. The little bead of water entered the canyon of my posterior.

"Come on, Julien, what is this crap?"

I didn't bother answering. I went to the shithouse to put the lid back where it belonged. While I was at it, I sat down on the throne to meditate.

"It's okay, Pierrot, excuse me, I'm all messed up. I don't know what's wrong with me. I'm happy for you, I really am, man."

We didn't discuss it again. I threw on some clothes as Pierrot boiled a couple cups of water. We mixed it with eight spoonfuls of coffee. We were in the mood to perforate our stomach linings in style.

"There's one more thing," Pierrot said. "I almost forgot."

"What?"

"Yesterday Sonia asked me if you really had something to do today, or if it was just an excuse to leave us alone."

"Really? And what did you say?"

"I said it was true, that we were throwing a party tonight."

"The perfect excuse, very good. What's the problem?"

"She invited herself."

Paradise is getting murdered by a burglar while you're peacefully marinating in your bath.

4

The doorbell rang; I rolled my eyes. I didn't really want to know how this whole thing was going to turn out. I glanced through the peephole. At the most I was expecting two or three girls with party hats and kazoos, but there was a whole herd of them at the gates.

I opened the door smiling.

"Hi there," said the girl who lived upstairs.

"Yeah, hi. Come in."

She went into the living room, followed by one girl carrying two small loudspeakers, another girl lugging the amplifier, then came the cassette player, the laser disk, more girls, and enough beer to float a battleship.

"Put all of that right here," Pierrot ordered. "There's a plug there. You can put the beer in the fridge, the bathroom's down the hall, and in case anyone asks, no, there's no guest bedroom."

"I hope I didn't invite too many people," the girl upstairs whispered to me.

"No, that's fine. The more there are, the more real it'll look."

"I don't think I've properly introduced myself yet. I'm Lisette."

She offered me her hand, which I shook limply.

"See the girl over there, with the white purse?"

"Yeah."

"That's Caroline, my best friend."

"That's nice."

I swear, we had had no choice in the matter. We had searched like crazy, but Bill and Paule were the only names that came to mind. We couldn't disappoint Sonia — she had to have her party even if it cost us an arm and a leg. Pierrot thought we should invite the woman upstairs.

"We don't even know her!"

"I know."

"That's crazy, Pierrot. I don't see why she'd want to spend an evening with total strangers. It's completely ridiculous."

Thirty seconds later, I was knocking on her door. She opened it. A couple dozen steps separated us. I had to move into the staircase to see her.

"Yes?" she said.

I knew she was in her early thirties; I'd met her a few times on the stairs. But we'd never spoken, not a word. When she opened the door, I thought she was pretty cute in her jeans and green sweater.

"I'm Julien," I called up, "your downstairs neighbour."

"Am I making too much noise?"

"Not at all."

She never made any noise, except when she had a certain male visitor. And even then, I just about had to climb up on a chair and glue my ear to the ceiling to follow their progress.

"Can I come up?"

"Why?" she growled.

Life in the big city! I don't know why, but over the last few years we've taken a turn for the worse. People have gotten completely off track — they can't even talk about the weather anymore. Guys like me, who have boundless trust in human nature, can't survive; we don't know how to adapt. You ask a little old lady for the time of day and you end up in jail for assault and battery. You smile at a kid and you pay for it with ten years for attempted kidnapping. It's gotten completely out of control. People think that if you talk to them, you're after their spare change, or you want to rob them blind and cut their throats. Distrust is to the city what manure is to the country: something in the air. It's become the city-dweller's best friend — after the revolver and the bars on the window, of course.

"I'd like to talk to you about something. It won't take long, and I think you'll find it interesting."

"I don't want to buy anything."

"Good, because I've got nothing to sell."

A miracle! There was a flash of white and I thought I saw the shadow of a glimpse of a beginning of an embryo of a smile.

"Okay, come on up, but only for a minute."

I took the stairs two at a time. She ushered me into the kitchen. There was a kind of pink soup in the sink. Her hands dove into it and fished out a pair of panties. The colour must not have been to her liking, since she sent the garment back into the solution. I felt like telling her that dyed underwear can give you irritations, but since the good Lord gave us each a toy to play with, He must not have wanted us to stick our noses into other people's. Or something like that.

"Do you want a beer?"

I was a little surprised. A few seconds before, she was about to scream bloody murder, and now she was all friendly, asking me if I wanted a beer and everything. Probably because I'd seen her panties. True, seeing a girl's underthings before you even know her name is a little unusual. Normally, that's the last thing you get to see. If you ever get to see it. Here I was, one foot in the kitchen and she'd already given me an eyeful. So why should I get all shy about it?

"Sure, that'd be great."

She shook out a few pretzels, and things began to look up. I felt like I could move mountains, pick up houses, and all kinds of other useless feats.

"We're having a little party tonight and I wanted to invite you. Since you're going to have to put up with the music, you might as well come downstairs. It's going to be fun, we're going to have loads of people."

Her eyes widened and her mouth hung open for a few seconds. "Funny, I was just looking for something to do. Can I come with a girlfriend?"

"Sure. And if you've got other friends who don't have anything to do tonight, don't worry, invite them, too."

"Two or three, maybe?"

"Sure. Two or three or fifteen."

She smiled and opened her eyes wide as she poured beer into my glass. All that as she scratched her left ankle with her right big toe. No doubt about it, that girl had perfect control over her muscles.

"No problem," she said. "I've got lots of girlfriends."

What worried me now was the quality, not the quantity. For a thing to really work, there has to be chemistry between the people. Everybody's waves have to agree to travel together for a few hours. Cliques can form — that's all right — and those cliques can even discreetly shit on other cliques — that's even better — but something has to happen: there has to be movement, things have to change. I hate those parties where everyone goes wandering miserably from one little group to the next, searching in vain for a spot to put down their glass and laugh a little.

I stamped on the floor three times. Half the mission was accomplished; now came Pierrot's part. To each his specialty. Mine was human relations, his was technical operations. We absolutely had to get our hands on some equipment, because what we had was closer to a gramophone than a stereo.

Four seconds later, he was knocking at the door.

"Excuse me," she said, moving towards the stairs.

I used the lull in the action to devour four or five more pretzel fragments and wash the whole thing down with a monster swallow of beer. The door opened and Pierrot asked if I was there. I finished off my beer, swept past my hostess, and headed for the stairway.

"We'll see you tonight! And don't forget, invite as many people as you want."

•••

I bulled my way into the kitchen to get my hands on a beer. A girl was squatting down in front of the fridge, scientifically stacking the seventy-two bottles. In the living room, the rest of them were busy connecting the red wire to the red terminal, the blue to the blue, and the green to the black, so we'd have some music before next year. Soon, Tom Waits started belching into our ears. That made everyone feel a lot better. Now that we didn't have to talk to each other to fill the silence, we could get down to some serious drinking. Personally, to get through all the bullshit that was going to fill the air tonight, I had to pay strict attention to my blood-alcohol level. Ideally, I'd avoid losing consciousness while achieving a certain degree of anesthesia. That way, everything that normally really bugs you slides off your back without a trace. You reach the detachment you need to let your irony show through when the situation calls for it. Which is no small advantage.

A long line formed in front of the fridge; the distribution of the bottles took place. I watched it all discreetly, smiling now and again, shaking a hand here and there, dropping a "Happy you could come" whenever a girl insisted on thanking me.

I pushed open the bathroom door and came face to face with Caroline, the girl with the white purse. She was sitting on the seat with her pants and her panties down to her thighs, trying her best to conceal her little private triangle.

"Hi," she said.

"Hello." I didn't know whether to leave, or stay and act unimpressed.

"I'm almost finished."

"Take your time."

I sat down on the edge of the bathtub and tried to find something else to look at. I drank a mouthful of beer, which kept me busy for a couple of seconds, then I nestled the bottle against my belly. She grabbed the top of her jeans, but they were so tight she had to twist and turn to get them back up where they belonged.

"Are those your pants?"

She bestowed a smile on me, then inspected herself in the mirror. I put up the toilet seat. She opened her bag and began touching up her makeup. I managed to piss, a few squirts at a time.

"My name's Caroline."

She extended her left hand. Naturally, my right was occupied, but my left was minding its own business, resting on my hip. I gave her a desultory handshake.

"I'm Julien."

"See you soon, Julien."

"Sure thing."

As soon as she went out the door, I slid the lock shut. How did I ever get myself into this mess? Before, when I made an ass of myself, at least I was smart enough to do it for a girl who was interested in me, not my roommate.

I washed down my face with a few litres of cold water and noticed how pale my skin was. A few nights' sleep — that's what the doctor ordered. Unfortunately, all I could do now was drink plenty of fluids. I gulped down the rest of my bottle.

In the kitchen, Lisette and Caroline had taken up position in front of the range and were salivating abundantly as they scraped off a few crumbs of hash. I felt madness taking hold of the premises; I headed for the living room. The place was full of girls dancing with their eyes closed, arms pointing towards heaven and hands sketching out a Hindu choreography. Pierrot was there in the middle of it all, as sober as a judge. He was leaning against the window, pretending to watch the action unfold, but I knew he was waiting for Sonia to show.

You'd have to have seen it to believe it. He'd come back from the upstairs neighbour's place, and no sooner had he got into the apartment than the phone rang. Of course he made a run for it. He didn't need to speak — just watching him make a dive for the receiver proved he was missing her already. We were headed down the slippery slope, and there were bad signs all around.

He produced a soft little voice I never knew he had. He whispered that it would be great if she came, that he couldn't wait to see her, that he'd spent a wonderful night, and all kinds of other sticky things. I pitied him, falling for a girl that way. On the other hand, I thought it was cool. If you don't have love in this life, you don't have anything at all. That's all I'll say about the subject.

"Come around eight-thirty," he cooed. "No, no, we have everything we need, don't bring anything . . . Me, too . . . See you soon."

We had a quick bite and Pierrot went sailing in the bathtub. I couldn't get a word out of him; his eyes were lost in the fog. I ran a rag over the greasiest stains in the kitchen. I lit a cigarette, opened the bathroom door, and sat down on the toilet. He sunk to the bottom of the bathtub with his fingers over his nose, then surfaced and made a face.

"Maybe there'll be a girl you like tonight."

Man always thinks that what's good for him is good for others, too. I raised my middle finger high.

•••

I zigzagged among the dancing girls, doing my best to avoid the flailing arms that whipped through the air past my nose and ears. The window ledge welcomed my butt, and I sat down across from Pierrot. We looked into each other's eyes to see what truths were there. He broke first.

"Well, man," he told me, "I never thought it would come to this, but our party is short on guys."

"It does look like a plot. But I never thought we could put together something so big so quickly."

"We're young, nothing can stop us."

"Yeah, but it won't last. We might as well use it while we can."

Lisette and Caroline came back into the living room. They'd put on dark glasses. I decided to go talk to them and check out their intoxication level. I carried out the operation stealthily, slipping along the wall, keeping a close eye on them. I wanted to find out what kind of mess I'd be getting into. They were laughing themselves silly, pointing at some of the dancers. Their laughter flowed from their guts, and they spat it into the air like miniature volcanoes. It shook them so hard that pretty soon they had to hang on to each other and lean their heads on each other's shoulders.

There's no defence against a laughing woman; her laughter is like a little butterfly rising from her soul, and no one can capture it. All you want is for it to continue, to keep on flowing. So you start working on perpetuating it, you bust your ass cracking her up twice a minute, and one fine day she tells you she likes you very much, you've made her laugh, but you're not serious enough for her. And good-bye.

I veered off towards the fridge.

"Innocent When You Dream" ended just in time for us to hear the bell. Pierrot made a dash for the door and the two lovers fell together. For a few seconds, the whole universe revolved around them. The rest of us became satellites and planets as they merged into a single majestic sun.

Sonia freed herself and I managed to catch her attention. She went down the hallway with Pierrot following involuntarily, as if he was attracted by her negative, considering how positive he was.

"Hi." Her lips delicately brushed each of my cheeks.

"You want a beer?"

"Sure."

I poured her a glass, then Pierrot gave her a tour of the apartment, starting with his room — and ending there, too.

I stretched out my legs on the kitchen table and waited. And waited. And drank. And drank. An hour later, I was pretty wrecked. Fortunately, Bill and Paule chose that moment to show up. A few minutes more and I would have missed them. Now I had the strength to make it through, if only I could skip a mouthful from time to time. Excuse my immodesty, but I do have a gift for it. When I reach the desired degree, I switch on automatic pilot and I can keep the momentum for hours without slacking off. After a while, it stops being centred in my brain. It turns into a generalized state of numbness that I can feel all the way down to my fingernails. A type of nirvana, you might say.

Which is probably why I suspected nothing when Paule invited me out on the back porch. Before Flo, I always let girls separate me from the group. It's stupid, but I always had high hopes at times like that. Nowadays, I flee that stuff like the plague.

She told me we should go up on the roof. Without Bill.

"Okay," I said, "but promise you won't make me do anything I wouldn't do normally."

"I promise."

Actually, I'd been looking for a fellow cliff-climber to go upstairs and philosophize under the stars. But I didn't want to ascend with one of Lisette's girlfriends. No sense hoping for Pierrot or Sonia — they were locked in the kind of serious discussion that should be outlawed on Saturdays. No room for cracking a few stupid jokes — you knew right off you weren't sailing on the same seas.

Paule took my hand and we ran up the stairs to the third floor. Air is a rare commodity at the turn of the millennium. Once on the balcony, we took the ladder up to the roof. She went first and I swear, I did everything in my power to refuse reception of the obscene messages sent by that thing in her pants.

The sky was as dark as a vat of methylene blue. We could make out a few tiny white lights twinkling in the distance and even a falling star, red and blinking. We sat our butts down side by side on the gravel roof. Our heels were propped against our backsides, our chins were on our knees, and our arms held the whole construction together.

We hadn't seen Bill and Paule for four or five months, but we decided to call them anyway. That's the way it is: you see each other, you don't see each other, it really doesn't matter. Paule hates going to bars, but she'd never say no to a house party. What do you expect — if Paule can't resist, Bill can't resist either. They stick together like glue.

Bill isn't his real name, but he won't tell us what it is. Paule knows but she's not going to spill the beans. I've got my own theory, since three of his brothers are called Romuald, Florient, and Jérémie. Bill must be the diminutive for Bilboquet or something like that. I like Bill, even if he does have yellow hair. It's true, I've never seen it before, a guy whose hair is actually yellow!

Paule, on the other hand, is fabulous. She's not only beautiful, she's got guts. And we have proof, seeing that Pierrot once had a thing with her. That's how we met her. They ran into each other in a bar (that's probably why she hates the places now). They hung out together for a while, then agreed to split up. They got along well, they never fought, but they never really loved each other. Hearing Pierrot's bedsprings squeaking night after night from midnight to three a.m., I wouldn't have said that. Anyway, they split up, no fights, no tears, they agreed it was best for everybody. I wasn't unhappy since Sophie had left me the week before, and, frankly, their noisy passion was beginning to torture me.

Besides, Paule couldn't stand Sophie, and naturally Sophie felt that Paule didn't appreciate her enough. Pierrot and I had to cook up a schedule to keep their meetings to a minimum. But it was inevitable: they ended up running into each other at the bathroom door for a midnight piss. To head that off, Pierrot spent a lot of time at Paule's while I stayed in the apartment. Sophie wouldn't have me at her place; she said I made too much mess.

Like I said, our affairs wound up around the same time. Pierrot stayed in touch with Paule, mostly by phone, while I kept up a relationship with Sophie's ass — by thought only.

A few weeks later, Pierrot showed us just how noble his soul was. Paule was telling him how she had nothing to do, so with no further ado, he introduced her to Bill, a guy from work who needed a little affection. Both of them were working for a bicycle courier company — Bill was using the money to pay for his computer course, and Pierrot needed the job to be eligible for unemployment insurance.

After their first date, Paule got on the phone and started calling us bastards, though we never did find out what had really happened. A week later, we caught them with their hands down each other's shirts, doing the usual dirty stuff. Us, bastards? Really?

I moved a little closer to Paule as the music wafted up to us like the smell of baking lasagna. Suddenly, I felt great. I didn't know whether the starry sky was to blame, or the girl next to me, but I felt like I could finally breathe.

"I'm happy for Pierrot. He deserves a little happiness," she said.

"Yeah."

"They look good together. I didn't have much time to check them out, but she looks like his kind of girl."

"I suppose."

Suddenly, despite the alcohol build-up in my blood, I noticed something had changed in her attitude.

"What's the matter?"

"Nothing."

"Say what you want, Paule, but I know you didn't bring

me up here to talk about Pierrot."

"I don't want to bore you with my problems."

"I came up here with you, okay? That means I'm willing to help. So trust me."

"It's about Bill."

I've always been able to keep my relationship problems to a minimum, but I've never managed to avoid other people's hassles. It just seems to work that way: as soon as something goes wrong, they all come running to tell me their story.

"Did he fuck up on you?"

"No, that's not it."

That's not Bill's thing, but you never know where love can lead you. Some guys even kill for it.

"What's the problem?"

"I want to have a baby, but Bill doesn't want to."

Uh-oh, quicksand ahead! Swampy terrain coming up! Watch out for booby traps! That's the kind of need men just can't understand. If a child is the extension of woman, then a beard or baldness would be the extension of man. It hasn't happened to me yet, but I know most women get around to it sooner or later. According to them, if you were born with a uterus, you've got to use it. Well, we were all born with tonsils but that doesn't mean we can't have them taken out. In any case, you can talk till you're blue in the face, it won't change a thing: the owner of a uterus who wants to take advantage of it is like a junkie needing a fix. You can tell her all you want that she's wrecking her life, she'll always get what she wants. Even if she has to pay a huge price.

The moon was laughing at us from behind a cloud of

flour. I felt like one of those guys in Acapulco about to dive from a high cliff for tourists, wondering whether to jump now or wait for the crest of the next wave. I tried to stall for time.

"Wait a second, I'm going to get a beer."

"You can have mine. I'm not very thirsty."

I took a couple of millilitres of consolation. "I'm sure it'll work out. You're both intelligent people, you'll find a solution."

"It's easy as far as I'm concerned. If he doesn't change his mind, I'll leave him."

For wine to turn to vinegar, it only takes a few hours.

"It doesn't work like that, Paule."

"I don't care about the rules, Julien. Why is the guy who says 'no' always right? Why do the weak keep the strong from moving ahead? Why do heroes always get shot because of cowards?"

"Can I tell you something, Paule?"

"What?"

"I don't understand a thing you're saying."

"Of course, you don't. You're a guy. You can't imagine what goes on in a woman's mind."

"I figured that out a long time ago. But you dragged me up here, and it certainly wasn't to demonstrate to me that I'm just another dense guy who can't understand anything about anything."

She started to cry; I started to shiver. I didn't know if I had anything to do with those tears, but I didn't want to risk looking insensitive. Especially since I'd already proved I was a moron.

"I'm sorry, Paule . . ."

"It's not your fault, Julien. I wanted to talk to you. I wanted you to tell me what you think. Sure, I'm afraid. I'm afraid having a kid will completely upset my life. I'm afraid I might be doing it for the wrong reason, but I'm more afraid not to have one at all."

I took her in my arms to try to comfort her a little. While I was at it, I stuck my nose between her neck and her shoulder. Jesus, it had been a long time . . .

"Listen, I don't want to hurt you, but I think you're completely crazy."

"I know."

Well, they say recognizing the problem is half the cure.

"If you want some male advice, give him more time. Guys need time to think things over, you know, a few months so the answer will come by itself. That way, we don't actually have to make a decision at all. It makes failure less bitter — if it fails. The thing we need is not to feel like the thing's being foisted on us from outside."

She smiled. I slipped my face back against her neck like a drunken boat in a sleeping marina. I took four or five deep breaths. Sated, I stretched out on the rooftoop, hands behind my head.

"I'm going down to talk to Bill."

"Good idea."

As she scurried down the ladder, Lisette and Caroline poured noisily into the street, followed by their herd of wombs. I closed my eyes for a few seconds and tried to think of nothing. It worked.

5

I counted exactly two hundred and eighty tiles on the kitchen floor, forty-nine metres of panelling around the apartment, and eight hundred and forty specks of cornmeal in a three hundred and forty-one millilitre box.

The mailman comes by at eleven forty-eight, give or take nine minutes. When the temperature hits twenty degrees, he puts on his bermudas. At twenty-five degrees, I suppose, he's naked underneath.

Last Monday, one thousand, four hundred, and fifty-two cars drove down my street between nine in the morning and nine at night. There are fifty-nine thousand definitions in the 1987 edition of my dictionary; it takes eighty-nine hours for dust balls to form under my bed. Pierrot has been gone one hundred and ninety-two hours and seventeen minutes. And I'm bored.

He really took me by surprise, the asshole. The possibility

had crossed my mind, but I never believed it would happen so fast. I'd just come back from the unemployment insurance office with this overwhelming urge to bash in someone's face. The bitch in charge of my file had cut me off. Apparently, I hadn't gone out and sucked up to enough prospective employers to prove I was seriously looking for work. Easy to say when your fat ass is nice and flabby from job security. Anyway, I figured, Pierrot's pulling the max, he'll be able to help me out until I can deal with the situation. Instead, I was heading straight for a brick wall.

When I arrived home, I found them sitting at the kitchen table. Pierrot hadn't set foot in the apartment for four days. We'd barely seen each other in the past two weeks. Sonia would come over and they'd take off right away. Usually, they invited me to join them, but I knew their hearts weren't in it. Who could blame them? Anyway, I was glad they were there so we could discuss my predicament.

As I moved down the hall, I pasted an idiot grin on my face so they'd think I was taking it okay. Strange, but when I broke the news, their faces fell. I never thought I had such sensitive allies. I asked what was going on.

"Nothing," Pierrot said.

"Don't take it the wrong way, it's not that bad. I'll be on my feet in no time. I just have to find something for a few weeks to shut her bureaucratic trap."

"That's not the problem, Julien. It just complicates our plans."

"There's nothing to it! Just spot me half the rent for this month, that's all. Really, Pierrot, it'll only be for a few days. You know when I look for a job, I find one. I can do anything that doesn't require an education. Think about it!"

I was revved up like an Olympic runner on steroids. Nothing could stop me now.

"I'm not worried about that, man. It's just that I had a plan, but now . . ."

"What's your plan?"

"I wanted to leave."

"When are you coming back?"

"Tomorrow."

"No big deal. Maybe I'll even have a job by then."

"I'll be back, all right, but just to pick up the rest of my stuff."

"What?" I asked, feeling the uppercut that was about to land.

"I'm going to live with Sonia."

I took a deep breath.

"Oh, I get it. Well, thanks anyway. Now, if you'll excuse me, I'm going to take a walk."

I headed slowly for the door. I could feel two sets of hangdog eyes fastened on to my back trying to keep me from going, but I desperately needed some fresh air. I went out the door and bolted for the stairs like a billy goat making for a she-goat's behind, but somehow I went down the last six stairs on my head and landed at the bottom wrapped around the pole that holds up the staircase. I ended up with skinned elbows and little bits of gravel stuck in my cuts. Even pride didn't stop me from turning back. I opened the apartment door, lowered my eyes, and exhibited my bloody elbows.

"I fell."

"Let me see," Sonia ordered.

She inspected my wounds attentively, then took a Q-Tip

and a little bottle from her bag. I didn't ask questions; I'd long since given up trying to understand her. She spread the stuff over my elbows. It was as soothing as a hammer blow on an ingrown toenail. Then Pierrot resumed the torture.

"There's something you have to understand, Julien."

I understood this: I'd wound up on my own with no money and a two-bedroom apartment on my hands.

"What?" I asked anyway.

"What just happened to you won't change our decision."

"Shit, you're impossible!"

We were going down a garden path with stupidities budding profusely around us. Soon, total pointlessness would burst into flower. Sonia hid for a few seconds behind her Q-Tip. Women have no tolerance for base natures.

"I'll leave you the food."

"Thanks, but without a fridge, it would spoil."

"I'm leaving the fridge, too. Sonia has one."

I decided to open a beer. I wasn't really thirsty, but I had to hold onto something. I lit up a smoke, too, to occupy my other hand.

"It's not the end of the world, Julien."

"Of course it's not."

I took a long swallow and said, "I know it's none of my business, but don't you think it's a little soon to be making a decision like that?"

"We've been together three weeks now."

"Well, in that case, you've known each other forever."

"She doesn't like being alone. She's not used to it."

"I come from a big family," Sonia piped up.

"And I want to manage her career."

I took a regal drag on my cigarette and blew the smoke into his face.

"You want kids, a deck, and a bungalow, too?"

His little eyes turned ugly and red. A sudden vision of hell emerged on our fair planet. Two little horns popped up on his head and a long rusty pitchfork pointed in my direction.

"I thought you'd understand," Pierrot said, jaw clenched.

I understood, all right. It was like a guy who leaves his girlfriend after eight years together, and when she starts to cry, he tells her, "Please, dear, don't make this any harder for me." Go ahead, Pierrot, strike while the iron is hot.

"I'm disappointed, Julien."

I glanced over at Sonia to make sure she hadn't hanged herself in the kitchen. She looked back at me, chagrined. I let her know that I really did understand what was going on, and that deep down, I didn't hold it against her. It wasn't true at all, but the message went out on its own. I'm like that. People could break into my house and steal my stuff and I'd still call out "thanks again" as I waved good-bye from the balcony. The important thing was to reassure Sonia. I knew her intentions weren't Machiavellian in the least. Unless she was totally twisted. Which was a possibility.

Pierrot looked disappointed at how things had turned out. He wanted me to drink deeply from the fountain of stupidity and make his life easier, but I had no intention of doing that. In any case, what difference would that have made?

One hundred and ninety-two hours and twenty minutes, now.

6

The staircase was made of wrought iron. From their frames, two doorbells watched me step onto the little balcony. I pressed the one on the right, knowing I had a fifty percent chance of being right. I'd been having good luck lately. I found twenty-five cents under the couch, left the house without forgetting my keys, and managed to cross more than forty streets without falling victim to a hit-and-run. Pretty unbelievable.

The door opened. I gazed upon my future benefactress.

"Hello, Madame."

"Hello. And how are you?"

"Getting by."

I fell into step behind her. The strong scent of cat litter tickled my nostrils. The pitch-black hallway was loaded with dull, outdated decorations. Finally, we emerged into a small living room bathed in ochre light. There they were.

Five of them. Identical. Monopolizing the entire couch.

"Hmm. Your cats are really something."

"Aren't they? Don't be shy, sit next to them. They adore company."

"Thanks, but I'll stand. I've been sitting all morning."

In fact, I'd just walked five kilometres, but I wasn't up to it. I've always found cats to be most appealing when they're lying squashed in the middle of the street.

"What can I do for you?"

"Listen," I said, "I have a bit of a problem. I'm not sure how to tell you. Uh . . . it's really stupid, and I know it's none of your concern, but . . ."

"Go on."

"The company I work for just fired twenty-four people. I was one of them."

"I see."

"So . . . uh . . . I don't think I'll be able to pay May's rent right away."

"Listen, we've seen each other once a month now for two years."

"Yes."

"I think we can consider ourselves friends, right?"

"I think so." My God, how could I sink so low?

"So," she went on, "you can tell me the truth. I was young once myself, you know."

Logic would say so. But it was still hard to believe.

"You're right. I can tell you everything. You've always been straight with me." A little bootlicking never hurts the down and out. "Actually, my mother is very sick and I wanted her to have a hospital room to herself. You know how expensive that is."

"I know," she sighed, lowering her eyes. "Is it serious?"

"She has cancer."

Silence. I felt I'd struck close to home. We both looked down at the carpet to indicate profound sadness. I shot a glance at the idiot felines crashed out on the sofa. Ten green eyes glinted reproachfully. Tapping all my powers of concentration, I telepathically informed them that cat meat is currently fetching twelve dollars a kilo in Chinatown.

"Sit down, let me get you a little pick-me-up."

She took two glasses from the shelf and disappeared into the kitchen.

"It'll do you good."

Scotch in the morning. As I took the first sip, I noticed the dexterity with which she placed the cap back on the bottle, and the finesse with which her wrist whirled it into place.

"My husband died of cancer, too."

"My mother's not dead yet."

"Excuse me, that's not what I meant. Really, I'm sorry."

"It's okay."

"How old is your mother?"

"Forty-four."

"So young! Are they going to operate on her?"

"Yes. Tomorrow."

"Wish her good luck for me."

"Thank you."

She snapped her fingers and the biggest of the cats jumped down, stretched, and leaped into the widow's lap. He sprawled out on her thighs and nuzzled the mauve polyester of her blouse. Her free hand slid down to the animal's neck and petted him there, where the skin was loose.

"His name is Henry," she said, smiling timidly. "Like my husband's."

It was all I could do to transform the fit of laughter that threatened me into a smile of compassion.

"Don't worry about the rent. I understand the situation perfectly."

"Thank you very much."

I got what I came for. I stood up, all smiles.

"You're leaving already?"

"Visiting hours start at two."

Something in her expression made me think I'd pay for my sins sooner or later. She got up, dislodging Henry, took my hands in hers, and looked into my eyes for an endless moment. Then she hugged me roughly. There was nothing fundamentally unpleasant about it — that is, if you eliminated the smell of cat piss, the whisky breath, and the kind of perfume they sell by the litre in gas stations.

"Be strong. If you need anything at all, please don't hesitate — just ask."

"Thanks again, Madame. If everyone in the world was as kind as you, things would be a lot better on this planet."

I didn't wait for an answer. The sidewalk was there where I'd left it, and I discovered that a Scotch after eighteen hours without food can really mess you up.

I jammed my hands into my jeans pockets and sauntered off lazily. Why rush? I wasn't working tomorrow, there was no one waiting for me at home, and even if it was lunchtime, I had nothing to eat. Poverty, solitude, and hunger bring you closer to that ephemeral notion called freedom. The sun was giving its all, the streets were empty, and I was filled with a sense of strength and calm, a serenity as solid as a rock — despite everything.

I picked up the pace a bit, trying to imagine what makes mankind live in these cement pigeon coops surrounded by neighbours. No wonder the balconies overflow with flabby, sun-starved flesh.

Behind an iron fence, one little house was squashed between two bulging buildings like a forget-me-not fighting to flower in a patch of dandelions. Two girls squatted on the ground, trying to smash a beer bottle. Unfortunately for them, Mama just poked her nose out the door. She moved towards them slowly and held out her arms at forty-five-degree angles. Immediately, the little girls grafted themselves onto each of her hands. It wouldn't make the papers, but the scene was strangely beautiful. A little house, three square metres of grass looking for some clean air to breathe, two kids, and a woman twenty-four, maybe twenty-five, years old. A microcosm green with health in a shit-brown universe.

Two offspring. Twenty-four or twenty-five years old. A terrifying thought. I know you have to start somewhere, but she really didn't choose the easy road. To take on that much responsibility, you really have to have serious backbone — more backbone than I have. But you have to get around to it sooner or later, man. You have to take a stand. After all, you can't spend the rest of your life shuffling down the same dead end. Twenty-six years, Julien, twenty-six long years hitched to the same falling star. Impossible — it has to be science fiction. I hurried off, chewing up the streets at a diabolical rate, pumped up like the sails of a galleon in a hurricane. I'd slam my fist into the first miserable face I saw, that's how much it hurt to be alive and laugh at death every step of the way. You skirt around things for years without ever acknowledging them, then, wham! they wallop you between the eyes. Twenty-six years old and I'm still dragging my feet, a black hole behind me and a black hole ahead. Twenty-six years, and all I've managed to salvage from the wreckage is a pair of jeans and a couple of T-shirts.

I looked to the right and saw cages. Cages to the left, too, with thousands of monkeys hanging frantically from the bars, hoping one day the doors will suddenly swing open. I had to get off this street and see something different. I stepped off the sidewalk and cut diagonally across the boulevard.

He was coming from the west. I heard him but I didn't feel like stopping. He was getting closer fast, his hand came down on the horn. In a split second, I clearly saw that life and death walk hand in hand, and that it doesn't take much for life to lose its footing.

Wheels locked and tires shed their skin on the asphalt. I found myself standing motionless on the white line in the middle of the street, nails digging into my palms.

"Are you blind or what?"

I gave him the finger. We glared at each other long enough to ignite a flicker of recognition. Funny, the day had started off well enough. All right, the last few minutes were pretty intense, but I'd seen worse.

"Hey, how about that?" Carrot-Top mouthed off for the benefit of his two passengers. "I think we know this guy."

I knew I shouldn't, I knew I'd pay dearly for it, but sometimes you have to seize the small pleasures life offers. I took a couple of steps towards the car. A beautiful

Volkswagen convertible. A 1990, probably. The best things about those cars are the mirrors. I summoned all my youthful strength, and, on contact with my shoe, the whole glass and plastic contraption went sailing through the air.

An alley branched off a few metres away. I hoped it would do the trick. I heard the guy shifting into reverse and, to be honest, it made me nervous. For some guys, a car is their reason for living. So imagine the bells that go off in their heads if you mess with it.

I bounded into the alley like a boar who's just realized where they're going to stick the skewer. It wouldn't be long before they caught up to me, but still I took the time to pick an iron bar off the ground.

The Volkswagen started sniffing my behind. I didn't bother questioning its intentions; I pressed myself against a telephone pole. They pulled up a few centimetres from me. I clutched the iron bar, and, with a spectacular swing, I brought it down hard on the right headlight. The whole socket exploded, shards of glass landing in my hair. That stopped things dead: instead of running after me, the three guys took time out to examine the extent of the damage. It wasn't until rage had worked its way up to their brains did they start to chase me. But I already had a good head start.

After a few strides, they decided to go back to the car. That was when I decided, out of some suicidal instinct, to up the ante. I turned around and followed them, and as they reached the car, I used the momentum of my run to hurl the iron bar in their direction. Everyone stopped to watch the object as it spun through the air with a whistling sound. Carrot-Top looked in my direction. There was such an expression of helplessness on his face that I almost wished the thing would stop in mid-air.

The bar touched down on the hood of the car, putting a dent in the metal only a few millimetres deep. Then it ricocheted and landed flat against the windshield. It was like tossing a pebble in a pond: we heard a *plunk* and saw the white circles spreading outward.

I took a right at the intersection and stumbled straight into the open-air market. The crowd would swallow me up. My lungs were burning, and every breath felt like I was gulping down fire. Like I figured, the shoppers who were peacefully going about their business couldn't have cared less about my pursuers.

I could hear them behind me. "Get out of the way, you assholes! Move it, lady!"

As I headed down the pedestrian walkway, their car drew up at the intersection and the guys got out. I ran like crazy past a few more stalls, but the muscles in my right calf were stiffening up. Not to mention my heart, drumming away in my ears. The three guys were dangerously close, but the crowd was denser in this part of the market, and I still had a second or two to think.

Behind his counter, sitting in the back of his truck, an old man gave me a toothy smile. He was getting a big kick out of it, one eye on the trio, the other on me. He even toasted me with his beer can. He was probably counting down the few seconds I had left to live. Cheers to you, too, you old fuck.

Florence, please, make a little room for me by your right side.

PART 2

7

I couldn't remember June being this bad. The heat was brutal, the humidity worse. Without an ice-water bath, I'd never be able to get to sleep tonight.

This was the sixth bottle I'd uncapped in two hours. My legs were complete jelly — from work as much as from alcohol. On my feet twelve hours a day, setting out crates of this, weighing out kilos of that. What a job!

When the old man had opened his truck door, I hadn't known what to expect. The metal squeaked and the sun cast its light on me. I was too dazzled to make out the expression on his face.

"It's okay, they're gone. You can get down. Bring a crate of cucumbers while you're at it."

I grabbed the crate and, a little disoriented, set my foot on solid ground like an astronaut stepping onto the moon with his groceries. The old man told me to put the cucumbers on the counter with the greener side up. I didn't ask questions; I was in no position to. Customers started coming up. He showed me where the money was, whispered the prices, offered me a beer.

When the rush was over, I thanked him for everything. He asked whether I was planning to come back the next day, suggested seven in the morning and handed me a few bills. I didn't dare count them. I told him thanks again.

I turned off the faucets. The water was lukewarm; I must have gotten the mix wrong. I staggered into the kitchen and came back with two ice-trays and emptied them into the bath. While I was at it, I cut a lemon into slices. They say there's nothing more refreshing than lemonade. Anyway, I have to find some way of using up what I bring back from the market.

I immersed myself in the waters, intent on spending all eternity there. I'd brought a few beers with me, which were now quietly drifting across the bottom of the bathtub.

The telephone rang. I stretched out my arm.

"Hello."

"Julien, it's Pierrot."

Shit, it had been a month. Thirty days. I was just getting used to it.

"Hey, Pierrot."

"How's it going?"

I've been burning the candle at both ends, knocking myself out to keep from thinking about girls, working seventy-two hours a week, and I can't take the heat . . .

"All right. How about you?"

"Great. I'm getting Sonia's things in order."

"That's nice."

"Yeah, I'm trying to figure out the major direction in her designs, a strong point I can sell. I plan to knock on a few doors, you know what I mean?"

"Sounds serious."

"It is. I'm going to put together a hell of a portfolio for her! They'll fall out of their seats. Those people are a bunch of yuppies who don't know their asses from their elbows, anyhow. You'll see, they'll cream over her stuff."

"How are they going to appreciate it if they don't know their ass from their elbow?"

"What are you trying to say?"

"Nothing."

My hand dove into the depths and discovered buried treasure. I brought it to the surface and unscrewed the cap.

"What about you, Julien, what're you up to?"

"I got a job selling vegetables at the market."

"That's good."

"Yeah. Well, it keeps body and soul together."

"Not bad for the women either."

"What women?"

"The ones you don't look at."

"Oh, I look at them. But I don't touch."

"Florence is gone, Julien. You'll have to get that through your head."

"Is that why you called? Because if it is, tell me and I'll hang up right now."

"I know you hate talking about it, but you've got to think about the present."

"You're right, I hate talking about it. Pierrot, you know the bullshit some guys'll go through for a woman. If I could avoid it, I don't see why I wouldn't."

"Is that for my benefit?"

"Forget it . . ."

"Okay, so I lost my head. But you know me, when I start something, I forget everything else. I'm like that, that's all."

"It's your life, Pierrot. You don't have to justify it. We're always twisting ourselves into a pretzel, so we might as well keep a few things simple. Besides, we don't owe each other anything."

Like a sledgehammer killing a fly. A piercing silence travelled down the phone wires the way a shiver runs down your spine.

"Maybe you're right, Julien."

If we ended the conversation there, we might never break down the barrier between us. But I just didn't have the strength for it.

"You see," he continued calmly, "I wonder what's going to happen in a few months. When the adrenaline's gone, when the passion cools down."

"You'll probably leave her, just like you left the other ones. But don't think about it. Let yourself go. Enjoy it."

No sooner is a hand held out than I'm busy shaking it.

"I don't think it's that simple. I've got to react, I've got to find something solid to hold onto."

"Maybe Sonia's the one. Maybe you'll never want anyone else. It could happen."

"Maybe."

Silence fell.

"Yeah," he said. "Maybe you're right. She could be the one."

Ciao, Pierrot, we'll see each other again someday. When your fine plans fall apart, when you've left Sonia, when I've lost my job. We'll meet again and pick up where we left off, and try to convince ourselves that we're not really losers, that anything's still possible. In the meantime, I'll work my ass off, so tomorrow night I can come home with my mind at ease, knock back a few brews, and put myself down for the count. The next day I'll go back to work and the next night drink the same beers. Next week — same thing. Until something interesting happens in my fucking life.

8

Most of the stalls were already set up, but a couple of trucks remained in the aisle. As I passed each counter, I gave a smile or a wave. Spirits were high this morning: after two weeks of sweltering heat, the weatherman finally promised a cooler day. Things can't stay rotten forever.

I stopped at the Fournier family stall, where Charlotte keeps the world's best coffee in her thermos. As usual, when we begin to chat and the black liquid starts galvanizing our brains, her parents give us a little space and pray that something might happen between us. Even though I'm a city boy, they figure our union could generate countless tons of potatoes.

At first I made a big show of resisting her. I adopted the strategy of the octopus and expelled my cloud of ink. Not to scare Charlotte off — but to blind myself: it was pretty easy; I just had to remember a few bad memories. Although

I did have to fight hard to keep from surrendering to that long hair and those twenty-year-old breasts and thighs.

The old man — I called him Granddad — was sitting in the back of the truck. Everything was ready; the counter was impeccable: all we needed was the first customer.

"Want a beer?" he asked.

"No, thanks."

He took the lid off the cooler and stuck his hand in.

"I'm a little late."

"You come when you want to. I'm in no position to ask anything from you."

True, some days I left here with twenty dollars in my pocket. Other days I might pull in sixty. But for some reason I felt like giving him my all. It had been years since I'd met someone who didn't feel he had to display all his knowledge, tell me his life story, and crush me with the benefit of his wisdom. What you really want from someone is to sit in companionable silence, bending an occasional elbow to bring a bottle to your lips as you watch the girls go by. If you can't do that, you haven't understood the essence of life. So when you finally meet a guy who thinks the way you do, you have to nurture him.

I leaned against the truck next to him. He looked up at the sky as he rolled a cigarette. In a flash, it was between his lips and he was striking a match. I stuck a ready-made in my mouth and used the same light. We stood like that, silent, drawing on our smokes like a pair of delinquents who siphon gas for kicks.

"What time did you get here this morning?"

"I slept in the truck. When I finish late like yesterday, there's no point spending an hour driving home, then heading straight back as soon as I wake up."

"No one's waiting for you?"

"No," he told me, grinding out his cigarette against the metal door. "What about you?"

I suppose I deserved that. Though I can't say his question surprised me. The old man has a particular interest in how young people live. It fascinates him to understand so little.

"No. When it comes to women, I've decided to keep the suffering down to what I really can't avoid."

"I understand. But it's not just suffering. It can be good, too."

"Experience shows that even under the best conditions, it ends up hurting. I'll leave that to others."

"Kids have less endurance today. As soon as a cloud appears, they send everything packing. It's a generation of quitters."

It's no accident that the old man is old. When he really wants to, he can pull out all the clichés in existence.

"What about the last woman you were with?" he asked. "Why didn't things work out?"

I stamped out my cigarette on the ground, cursing all the saints in heaven.

"For reasons of mortality."

"Oh."

What can you add to that?

"My wife is dead, too."

Well, he added.

When he said the word "dead," I heard a sense of relief in his voice. Like liberation after years of imprisonment. I should have changed the subject, but I couldn't.

"How long's it been?"

"A month."

There's nothing more intriguing than an open wound. I was afraid I wouldn't be able to resist the temptation to ask how, why, and how old, but fortunately for him, an old lady decided to visit our stall. Granddad got down from the truck, hitched up his pants, and went to serve her.

"Yes, ma'am, what can we do for you?"

"Sorry to bother you," she said in a wavering voice, "but I'd like to know. Your green grapes, are they seedless green grapes?"

"Yes, ma'am, the best seedless green grapes in the market."

"Can I taste one?"

"Of course, go ahead."

She picked a few grapes from a bunch as another woman, who was much younger, approached the other side of the stall. My eye fastened on to her immediately, partly out of curiosity, but mostly because I've always been partial to women in jeans and a T-shirt. I waited for her to ask to be served, but she started helping herself. First a bunch of red grapes, then a bunch of purple ones went directly into the bag slung across her chest. Of course Granddad saw nothing. Then both her hands sank into the Moroccan tangerines, and she grabbed a canteloupe and added a couple of bananas, why not? I've always been more on the side of the thief than the cop, but still, that was my salary she was stealing. I wavered uneasily between jumping in and letting it slide, like a tightrope walker looking to regain his balance with a cocktail umbrella.

She didn't notice me until I'd jumped down from the back of the truck. I tried to put on an unconcerned air and not tip my hand. She smiled. I took that as a good sign. Then she ran like hell.

I leaped over the counter and rushed after her as Granddad looked on, astonished. Quicker than I was, she carved a passage through the crowd while I careened into customers and displays, leaving a trail of upset fruits and vegetables.

At the main aisle, she cut left and out of my line of sight. I heard a furious car horn and the squeak of brakes. By the time I reached the corner, a curious mob had gathered around the car.

"Get out of my way! Move it!" I yelled, waving my arms wildly.

I managed to weave my way to the car. I knelt down next to it and discovered a long red streak underneath. It led to a large flattened pomegranate by the back wheels. I got out of there.

"Get out of my way. Move it!"

She had gotten a good lead on me, thirty metres, maybe. I gave it all I had. Sprinters of the world, watch out! I blazed across the parking lot like a trail of napalm. The body has its limits, though, and mine appeared pretty quickly, especially around gut level. Fortunately, she seemed to be running out of gas, too.

At the exit to the market, by the boulevard, I made one last push. Stretching my arm as far as it would go, I lunged and grabbed the bottom of her T-shirt between two fingers. Our gallop slowed to a canter, then abruptly ended in an anarchic set of dance steps.

"Listen," I said, my heart in my throat. "I don't know . . . I don't know why I chased you . . ."

We caught our breath, my hand still on her T-shirt, pulling it tight across her chest and revealing her magnificent wares. "Seriously, I don't give a shit about the fruit."

"Well, what do you know, neither do I!"

And with that, she took her bag by the bottom and spilled out its contents. Dozens of multicoloured fruits rolled and bounced along the boulevard. I acted as though I didn't get the message.

"Honestly, I don't know why . . . I just know that . . . that I was really afraid when I heard that idiot slam on his brakes."

"Shut up!" she growled, giving me a crushing look.

I should have just left. But the sight of those eyes as dark as plums made me rush headfirst into the void.

"Okay, let's forget about it . . . Sorry, it wasn't right . . . I shouldn't have chased you."

I was completely losing my head. Another minute and I'd be apologizing for having been robbed. For a guy who'd given up girls, I was having trouble letting go. I let loose of her T-shirt, which was a start. Once she was free, she took off. At an incredible pace, considering the race we'd just run. My side knotted up with a fierce stitch, I trotted along painfully after her like a little chick trying to catch up to its mother.

"Maybe," I ventured, "it was just a way to start a conversation."

"Fuck off, shithead!"

I stopped. She didn't. There's something terribly beautiful about a woman walking away. I know, I've seen my share.

"I guess you don't feel like going for a beer." Really,

Julien, try to maintain a shred of dignity. "Even if I'm paying?"

She didn't turn around. She kept putting one foot in front of the other, heading in the wrong direction.

9

A painful awakening. Black coffee and despair. Then the market. Good morning, Charlotte; hey, Granddad.

"Want a beer?" the old man greeted me.

"Can't you drink orange juice like everybody else?"

"Uh-oh. I see we're in for another beautiful day."

It was true. For the last three days I'd done nothing but bitch. Three days spent contemplating my life as I felt the noose tighten around my neck. Even with all the experience I'd had at staying clear of women, I couldn't get this one out of my head. I'd only just managed to convince myself that I could build a quiet little life solid enough to withstand the storm, and wham, she hit me like a ballistic missile.

At least if I'd let her steal the damn fruit, she might have returned. At least if I'd kept my mouth shut, I might have been able to see her again. But no, I had to poison my sorry existence with the memory of the way her shoulders rolled as she moved away — never mind the picture of her amazing ass. Compared to hers, Sophie's was a sad-looking butt with neither shape nor firmness, a kind of meaningless bulge. Hers, on the other hand, was the eighth wonder of the world, sculpted out of the rock of the Parthenon, as muscular as marble, but as hot as blood. An earthy ass, a thoroughbred ass, an ass of unique vintage, bubbling over with life itself like an underground spring.

Eleven, noon, six o'clock. The old man was crashed out, his head resting on a crate in the back of the truck. I shucked a few ears of corn to inspire the customers. The heat was back, and the guy on the radio said it was beating all records since 1932. This must be what hell is like: thirty-five degrees in the shade with no hope of rain.

Suddenly, it seemed like a blanket of silence had been thrown over the market. The shouts of the merchants, the rustling of plastic bags, the coins jingling together — just like that, it all stopped. I looked up and there she was, standing in the aisle, wearing the same jeans and T-shirt, moving slowly in my direction. Time screeched to a halt, freezing everything but my heart as it raced after life and caught up to it somewhere in my inner ear. She was standing there with her tangled mop of hair, her ripe-fruit eyes, her magnificent ass. She was standing there. Shit, what was I supposed to do?

"Hi," she said, raising her eyes.

"Hi," I answered, lowering mine.

"I'd like a kilo of red grapes."

I acted like it was no big deal, as if I hadn't spent the past seventy-two hours cursing the day we'd met, hadn't rampaged through the entire city trying to overcome hellish insomnia, hadn't dreamed of being run over by a truck on the corner of Lonelyhearts Boulevard.

"A kilo? Coming right up," I said, dumping two bunches on the scale.

The needle wavered for a moment. Even the milliseconds seemed to last forever.

"That'll be four seventy-five . . . if that's okay."

"Yeah. I've got the cash."

"Great," I said, reaching over to the pile of bags. "Are you going to eat them here or pour them out on the street?"

It was a pretty good battle, but unfortunately, we'd both end up losing if we kept it up. Her eyes wouldn't let go of me; they seemed to shine brighter and brighter.

"I'll eat them here — with a beer, if possible."

Of course it was possible. Except that, for the time being, I was impaled by her eyes, barely able to speak the words that squeaked out from between my dry lips.

"It's possible. Sure, it's possible."

I invited her behind the stall and we hopped up into the truck. I didn't know where to look. I felt like Adam faced with the forbidden fruit, wondering whether his teeth were up to it.

"I'm really surprised to see you again," I said.

"Yeah?"

"But happy! Surprised, but happy."

"Yeah?"

"Why'd you come back?"

"No reason. Can we talk about something else?"

"If you want. But I'm still surprised you came back."

"Enough already."

Not as easy as I thought. I tried another tack.

"You live around here?"

"Yeah, in the red brick building over there, above the butcher."

"Why didn't you run there the other day?"

"I don't feel like talking about that."

"Well, I don't live far either. You go two streets over, turn left, and it's just four blocks down."

"What's the number?"

"Sixty-three seventy-seven. You know, I don't know how to say this, but . . ."

"You haven't stopped thinking about me since the other day."

She was quick, too.

"That's it."

"My ass has that effect on everyone."

"No, no, it's not your ass, it's you."

"Yeah, you know me so well."

"I know I don't know you . . . but I'd like to." I was digging my own grave. I prayed for a moment's respite. If she kept shooting wildly that way, she'd end up hurting somebody.

"Sure, you'd like to know me naked is what you'd like."

Shot in the heart.

"You should come and steal at night," I told her, changing the subject. "It's a lot easier."

"Don't worry, I won't come back. I've got nothing against you."

"Against who, then?"

She smiled. A mouth lined with strong, straight teeth — a natural wonder. I didn't hesitate: I showed her my own pearly whites.

"We'll talk about that some other time, okay?"

"Okay. By the way," I said, holding out my hand, "I'm Julien."

She delicately slipped her hand into mine as I tried to figure out how many personalities inhabited her body.

"I'm Annie."

Granddad had already started clearing the shelves. I had no choice but to get in gear and load the truck.

"I'm sorry, Annie, but I have to give him a hand. That's what he pays me for."

"No problem. I should get going anyway. We'll see each other some time."

I wasn't about to let her get away again and sentence myself to hell until her next appearance.

"If you insisted," I told her, "I might be convinced to go to your place for a beer."

I admit it lacked subtlety, but I was a little rusty.

"I'm afraid that wouldn't be possible, Julien."

I guess you can't ask for too much from a single day. Happiness is like Chinese water torture: it takes forever to flood you completely.

"On the other hand," she added, "there's nothing stopping us from going to sixty-three seventy-seven."

10

"Now I see why you have to steal to eat."

We'd put away a couple of beers, then got it into our heads to make a vegetarian pizza. Naturally, I had everything we needed on hand. I ate a medium-sized piece and watched while she devoured the rest.

"Isn't there a good movie on tonight?" she asked.

It wasn't exactly what I had in mind, but it was better than having her leave.

"Yeah, there's one with Marlon Brando."

It was a flick from the fifties or early sixties, the story of a biker who falls in love with a waitress in a greasy spoon. I'd seen it more than once, but didn't mention that. Actually, I've seen all the movies seven or eight times. Except for the ones they never show on TV. We settled on the couch with a good metre between us. We had talked a little over dinner, but hadn't really gotten to know each other any better. I didn't find out what she did or where she came from, and I couldn't get her to talk at all about what had happened the other day. Right now the only thing we had in common was the case of beer propping up our feet. It was her idea to bring it into the living room so we wouldn't have to get up every time. I appreciated the sentiment.

"Looks pretty good," I said, a few seconds into the movie.

Annie nodded ever so slightly; she was completely entranced by the credits. Commercials were invented for people like her, to keep them from falling into a cinematographic coma. Time out for Preparation H, Ex-Lax, and Tampax. I'd always wanted to meet the idiot who claimed advertising was the mirror of society.

The movie started up again. Annie's head pivoted forward a few centimetres. I tried to think of a subtle way of getting her attention.

"Want a beer?"

I thought I detected the slightest bat of an eyelash. Jubilant, I dug into the case, took out two, and used the bottom of my T-shirt to twist off the caps without shredding my palms.

"Quiet!" she ordered.

Pitifully, I handed her a bottle and downed half of mine in a single swallow. But there was a god for lovers after all: the first time Brando appeared on the screen she slumped back in disappointment.

"Oh, no. I've seen this one before."

I flipped through the channels nervously, trying to find something worth watching. Her presence depended on it. After three fruitless turns of the dial, I came back to Brando.

Annie leaped up and disappeared into the hallway. I had this horrible feeling she was getting her stuff together, but didn't dare go in search of visual confirmation. Brando looked on top of the world on his bike, but just you wait, Marlon, when you meet that waitress and she'll fuck you up so bad you'll run away clutching the handlebars of your Harley like a child holding onto a toy. I myself would stay and fight, but obviously we weren't in the same league.

Annie reappeared in the doorway with just her T-shirt on. Mercifully, it came down to her thighs.

"What are you waiting for?" she said.

"Uh, I dunno."

"Scared of me?"

"Of course not."

"Well, then, move it!"

Timidly, I took her hand and followed her into the bedroom. We stood by the bed: Annie in her T-shirt, me in my nerves. Sex is slippery ground. Not unpleasant, but slippery. She came closer and kissed me softly, to calm me down maybe. Then she moved away, and all her heat remained with me. I was as excited as a dog that's just dug up a mammoth bone.

She looked me over with a strange expression in her eyes.

"I'll give you ten seconds to take off your clothes. If you can't do it, I'm leaving."

I laughed and wondered what kind of crazy woman I was dealing with.

"Come on, I'm timing you. Go!"

I started with my shirt, as my right foot kicked off my left shoe and my left my right, then I moved down to my belt, pulling the pin out of the hole and pushing the buckle out of the way. I unbuttoned my jeans and put one hand on either side to pull everything down. My left leg went up and out of my pants, then back down to give the other one a chance. Satisfied with my performance, I gazed upon my executioner with victorious eyes.

"It took you eight seconds but you forgot the socks. If I'm generous and give you a second a sock, that'd be exactly ten seconds. Congratulations."

She grabbed the bottom of her T-shirt and lifted it over her head. Sweet Jesus! Sometimes life shows you such incredible beauty that you don't know where to look. Speechless, motionless, I just wanted to open up a beer, sit down, and gaze at her until the year two thousand.

"Well, what are you doing?"

"Looking at you."

"There's nothing to look at."

Thirty centimetres separated us, but it might as well have been the entire universe. It was driving me crazy. We sat down on the bed. I didn't know where to start, though I had a terrible urge to bite into her and rip out a chunk of flesh. My brain was completely numb, but my cock was going full force.

She turned her back to me; I wouldn't have the privilege of seeing her face. Another secret. I let my eyes, and then my hands, take in the spectacle of her shoulders, her back, the top of her ass. She must have felt me breathing; little shivers started at the base of her spine and rippled up to her neck. I folded my arms around her breasts and drew her close, resting my head on her shoulder. Our necks crossed like swords.

Her lips glistened like a raspberry in the morning dew. I picked them. I picked all the rest, too, counting the seconds of my happiness like the beads of a sacred rosary.

11

My eyes like slits in the torrential rain, I walked gloomily to the market. I had scoured the apartment in a panic, telling myself that it couldn't be true. I'd found nothing, not a shadow of a woman or a hair of regret, no note on the bedside table, no lipsticked message on the bathroom mirror. Impossible — that girl kept slipping through my fingers. Just when the wind was starting to blow my way, just when I thought I stood half a chance, she packed up her soul and her ass and split without a backward glance.

I finally resigned myself to the obvious, put on my jeans and T-shirt, and searched like an idiot for my keys. I couldn't find them, of course, because of the dense layer of fog between my brain and reality. I left without locking the door, cursing heaven for letting me fall back into the feminine trap.

Charlotte understood instantly that I wasn't at my best,

but she didn't bug me about it, for which I thanked her silently. Her coffee was as cold as the day. I swallowed it in two gulps as the sympathy written in her eyes spread a little warmth on my frozen shoulders. Shitty life.

Granddad was behind the counter, a pocket knife in one hand, a carrot in the other. He was coolly whittling what looked like a little shotgun.

"Hey, there," he mumbled without looking up.

"Hi."

"So? How'd it go?"

I told him the whole story, and the idiot burst out laughing like a carnival gypsy. I could even tell you how many fillings he had.

"And she left before you got up," he repeated, scratching the back of his head. "She needed to sleep with someone. Didn't matter who."

He folded the blade of the knife and said slyly, "Either that, or you fuck like a dying turtle."

He slipped the knife into his back pocket and tried to conceal a gleeful smile.

"On the other hand," he concluded, "maybe she goes to work early."

Christ, let it be the job!

The old man bit into his shotgun, a smug grin twisting his face, which I would have gladly pummelled with a couple of watermelons.

"Anyway, Julien, don't you think the girl's a little strange?"

"No, why?"

"I don't know. She's just not completely normal. For starters, she steals."

"Come off it! Everyone does, to one degree or another."

"Maybe, but most people don't go off for a beer with the guy who catches them."

"That's because she likes me, damnit! You really want to take that away from me, don't you?"

"If that's the case, why didn't she want you over at her place? It's right next door."

"How should I know? Maybe she has an asshole roommate or a retarded brother she doesn't want people to meet."

"Or a husband. There's something fishy about it. She's not telling you the truth, Julien."

"She's a little lost, that's all. Maybe she's been hurt. She just needs someone to take care of her, pay a little attention to her."

"I don't think she's as lost as all that. I get the feeling she knows exactly where she's going."

I looked over at the red brick building, and let me tell you, it was seriously starting to bug me. If I was being manipulated, I wanted to know about it. I've got nothing against people using me, so long as they tell me first. After all, it's the polite thing to do.

"I'll be back in fifteen minutes."

I crossed the market with a manly stride, rain and sweat spraying off me as I attacked the stairs leading up to the first floor. I leaned on the bell; ten seconds later, the door buzzed an answer. I opened it and pasted on my most charming smile. Up the stairs, a short-haired brick shithouse was waiting for me. It wasn't his square jaw or his immense thighs that were wider than my chest — but a little something told me he was a criminal, the brutal type.

It was unmistakable — I get the same feeling every time I see someone in a police uniform.

"Yeah?"

"Sorry, I must have made a mistake. I was looking for a girl, but I think I've . . ."

"You looking for Annie?"

It was ridiculous, but I found the guy's composure reassuring. In all humility, I do have a certain flair for sniffing out people I can trust.

"That's right, Annie."

"Wait a second."

Just like I thought: she had a retarded brother she was ashamed of. I stood there frozen on the staircase asking myself what a girl like that could be doing with a cop. It's amazing how wrong you can be about people. You think you know them, you know what they like in bed, and what they whisper at the crucial moment, but you'd never guess they had a weakness for the cop class. Strange world.

I heard a loud crash and looked up just in time to see the guy tossing a dresser from the top of the stairs. The thing hesitated over the first few steps, then started jumping over them and picking up speed. I ducked out of the doorway as the behemoth crashed onto the porch, ripped off the old wooden railing, and flopped onto the sidewalk one floor down, casting up roostertails of water.

"She was supposed to pick up her clothes a week ago. Give her the message."

I didn't ask for details; I ran down the stairs before he could bring out the piano. The sidewalk was littered with mangled, splintered pieces of wood. Hurriedly, I gathered up the clothes trapped in the dresser's carcass, like a grave robber going about his sordid business. I stuffed everything I could into my T-shirt and bundled the rest in my arms. Maybe because I had her clothes snug against my belly, acting like some telepathic link, but as I made my way back to the stall, I felt I was beginning to understand what she was up to.

•••

When I got back to my apartment, I checked out every room to make sure nothing had moved. My keys were waiting for me under the kitchen table. Brilliant. I dropped Annie's clothes on the bed and thanked heaven for the few moments of happiness awaiting me. First I turned to the T-shirts; I'd start with what was less intimate. They were red, which didn't really surprise me. Annie was a ball of fire, a comet, a supernova that refused to burn out. I laid each of them out flat to gently smooth away the wrinkles. Then I folded the little sleeves onto the breasts, swallowing hard. Just at the shirts and already I was as tortured as a horny saint wearing steel-wool underwear. I ran to get a beer. God, it was good to be alive!

I moved on to the camisoles, a diabolical invention meant to separate pessimists from optimists: the former believe they hide half of what they want to see, while the latter think they actually reveal it. A pink one, five red ones, and a looser black one I wanted to see her bend over in. I was suffocating — I quickly swallowed a mouthful of beer.

On to the underwear. My God! Women's underwear fairly exhales life, covered with blooming flowers and little beating hearts. Sure, beyond a certain size, the flowers wilt and the hearts develop angina, but that wasn't the case here.

This girl's ass was so small the underwear didn't even fit on my head. I know, I tried.

When the exercise was over, I put everything meticulously into the closet. As I stepped past the mirror, I heard a little voice inside saying, "What're you doing, Julien? You're feverish and sweaty, and spinning in circles like a madman waiting for her to come back. What happened to all your fine resolve? Your noble promises? Where are your balls?"

I slid under the covers and pitifully sniffed my way across the pillow, hoping to find a few threads that still retained her scent.

•••

Ten o'clock. I let the old man in on the latest developments. I even told him my theory. He thought it was interesting, but still bet me ten dollars I was wrong. I climbed up into the truck, gave him a wave, and drove through the market into the street. I was so happy I caught myself dreaming about a certain Volkswagen, now that I was behind the wheel of two tons of steel.

I drove slowly, taking apart and putting back together the damned jigsaw puzzle. Each piece looked to be in its right place, with an impeccable logic. I parked the truck in front of sixty-three seventy-seven. I was completely in knots — my legs, my head, and, most of all, my heart.

The door was unlocked. I opened it as quietly as possible and inched down the hallway, careful to step over the creaky floorboards. Outside the bedroom door, I leaned against the wall to let out the breath I'd been holding since I entered the apartment. I could smell her. I knew she was there. Just as I had come to know the smell of death at one point in my life, today I recognized that of the abyss. Deep down I knew we were going to jump, and when we did, we wouldn't be able to climb out again. Florence, goddamnit, why'd you let me do this?

I poked my head into the room. She was lying peacefully on my bed. I'd won the bet, but sometimes there's something terrible about being right. I was literally frozen to the spot; this slip of a girl tangled up in my sheets, her little fists pulled up against her, knocked the legs out from underneath me. Even sleeping, she was full of life. There's no rest for girls like her. They work night and day just to live a little, to grab a couple good mouthfuls off life's buffet. Suddenly I felt like crying; I knew I wasn't up to it. I'd never be able to make a girl like her happy. I didn't have what it takes, the little motor that keeps on forging ahead, pushing harder and harder without a thought for the consequences. Even the minimum requirements for getting through life eluded me. I took the punches, I sucked it in, it looked like I was holding my own, but inside it was tough. The smell of rot was taking over.

Then, damnit, she opened her eyes. It took her a moment to realize she was cornered. I was ashamed of myself. She gave me the exact same smile she had when she was shoplifting. I took up a solid position in the doorway; she wouldn't get away this time.

"Hi," I said.

She sat up slowly on the bed. "You want me to leave, I suppose."

For once she wasn't on top of the situation. For once I didn't feel totally out of it. After all, I'd figured out what she was up to.

"Don't you want to know what I'm doing here?" she asked, casually running a hand through her hair.

"No, I know."

"I didn't steal anything, I just slept."

"I know."

"You must be wondering how I got in."

"You took my keys yesterday and made copies. You spent the day here, then you left before I got home and put my keys under the table."

She closed her eyes. I stood there, up to my knees in uncertainty.

"I also know that your boyfriend kicked you out."

She lifted her eyelids slowly and shot me a damning glance. "What do you mean?"

"I went by your place."

"I knew I fucked up when I told you where I lived. I should've kept my mouth shut. I knew I couldn't trust you."

It was like a knife blade slipping between the bone and the flesh. I began to think the old man was right. Suddenly I felt exhausted and wished I'd never taken up the battle and wasted a year of abstinence.

"I brought you back some clothes," I said. "They're in the closet."

Completely naked, she got up to check. The sight deflated me.

I put my cards on the table. "I thought the fact that you'd chosen my apartment might have something to do with me."

She took the time to look me over, evaluating me from head to toe, as if she had to choose her next words very carefully. "I knew you wouldn't pull any bullshit if you found me."

"Yeah, I'm known for being a soft touch in situations like this. I have a tendency to trust people. It doesn't pay off very often, but what can I do? I'm a fool that way."

"It's not so foolish," she mumbled, stuffing some clothes into her knapsack.

My fatigue was nearly unendurable. Even the energy born of desperation had deserted me. I threw in the towel.

"Excuse me, Annie, but I have to get back to the market. In any case, you don't need me anymore."

"Wait a minute, Julien."

"What? You want a bite to eat before you leave?"

The words slipped out by themselves. Her answer was spontaneous.

"Fuck off, shithead!"

Her tone was so violent I couldn't answer. I gave in a little further.

"Okay, well, I'm off. Don't forget to close the door on your way out. And if it's not asking too much, leave your keys on the table."

I made it out of the room, but the hallway was too long and she had time to catch up with me.

"At least let me explain. I did something stupid; one of his buddies caught me stealing in a drugstore. When he found out, he gave me ten minutes to get out of the house. I've been sleeping anywhere I can for a week now. I'm not trying to make excuses, I just want you to know I've got nothing against you. I can be an idiot myself sometimes."

She was completely caught up in her own self-destruction, but I couldn't stand to watch her fall.

"He's the idiot."

Slowly I felt the distance she'd always kept between us

begin to evaporate. I could see something in her eyes crack and splinter, then dissolve. She took a step towards me; it was the only thing left separating us. I knew full well I wasn't strong enough. I knew I was walking the plank with no land in sight, but I held her tight, and we clung desperately to each other like the sole survivors of a nuclear winter. Not to warm one another — just to stop the dying a little.

12

The old man was in great shape. We worked until seven, laughing the whole time, then loaded everything up. He had decided to close the stall for a few days, something he hadn't done in a long time. He looked younger as the day wore on. Every second was another shovelful in the tunnel of the great escape.

The three of us climbed up front — Granddad at the wheel, Annie in the middle. The old truck extricated itself from the market, sputtered all the way to the highway, then dove into the fast lane in a cloud of blue smoke.

After a few kilometres, Annie's head fell onto my shoulder. We spent an hour that way, having our butts bounced around and our shoulder blades shimmying. I didn't care. If that was the price of having her with me, I'd pay the bill in cold cash. After ten months of belief in abstinence with blind faith, I had to admit the entire undertaking had failed miserably. Florence's death should have immunized me, but I'd returned from celibacy as weak as ever, and I felt myself diving, head down, back into the same hangman's noose.

We turned onto a small gravel road and an imposing dust cloud raced along behind the truck, giving it the grandeur of a horse-drawn Trojan chariot. At the end of the road, a small patch of green began to spread back until it cut deeply into the horizon.

"What you see here," the old man whispered, "is what I use as a workshop and a chicken coop. That's where I keep my cow."

I could just picture him in the morning in his long johns with the trap door, sauntering out of the house to scare up a couple of eggs and squeeze a few squirts of milk into his coffee.

"What about all those fields, what do you grow there?"

"Nothing. It's too big, too much trouble. I buy everything from another farmer. That's my only crop over there — potatoes. That's it."

"Yeah, but you make less profit that way, don't you?"

"Sure, but I'll live longer."

The truck came to a stop under an old oak tree and let out a sigh of relief.

"We're there already?" Annie asked, opening one eye. "That was painless."

She rubbed her eyes. I rubbed my shoulder, then opened the truck door and planted my heels in the dirt. Granddad got out and inhaled a few deep breaths of clean air, looking up at a delicately purple sky. Aside from the song of a cricket or some other insect, there wasn't a sound, just dead silence. Even the oak absorbed the breeze in silence. Too much oxygen and tranquillity all at once can be dizzying for someone who's never been out of the city. We ran for shelter inside.

"Go take a look upstairs. You'll be sleeping up there."

Annie ran for the staircase, grabbing my hand on the way, and I swooped and spun along behind her to the top. We stood in a large room covered with little blue flowers. The first thing I noticed was the imposing brass bed. Annie couldn't resist; she threw herself onto it and disappeared underneath the covers. She emerged looking happy, so I smiled, too.

"Did you see the fireplace, Julien? And the private bathroom?"

"Yeah."

"I've never seen anything so beautiful. I'd stay here any day."

If I could live with her, I thought, I'd even move into a rundown hut in a village of cannibals.

We got our stuff from the truck and went back upstairs, throwing everything into the dresser. When we opened the drawers, a spicy scent wafted out like some forgotten genie. Annie took the two top drawers and I got the bottom ones, but as soon as her back was turned, I put my underwear in to snuggle next to hers.

•••

While Granddad and Annie were in the barn, I cleared away supper, then wiped the table and counter, thinking the whole time about how empty the bedroom had felt. I had a strong suspicion the old man hadn't set foot there since his wife died. I'd done the opposite after Florence's death. I visited all the places we'd been together, as though covering the stations of the cross.

The door opened and Annie rushed in.

"Julien! I milked the cow. You should've seen it!"

"She's a pro," the old man confirmed, putting the milk jug in the fridge.

Obviously, she only had to try her hand at something once to put to shame all those who'd devoted years to the task.

"That's not all," she went on, "I renamed the cow."

"What?"

"Dalida."

"Dalida the singer?"

"Yeah. I swear they have the same eyes."

•••

A torrential sun flooded into the room. Annie was glued to my side. It must have been forty degrees where our bodies touched. Ever since we'd started sleeping together, as soon as one of us opened an eye, the other would wake up a few seconds later. We didn't want to waste a single minute.

We mingled morning breath before clambering downstairs. Annie judged by her appetite that it must have been about nine o'clock. Granddad served us chicken eggs, pork bacon, and wheat-flour bread. A single cloud cast its shadow over the table, but it was a big one: there was no more coffee.

•••

I turned right at the paved road, like the old man told me

to. All the windows were down, there was a breeze, there was Annie, and that was enough to make me smile as I ate up the dotted white line. By the time we made it into the village ten minutes later, the arm I'd been hanging out the window was just about cooked through. The village itself looked like a quaint place to come to die. In fact, they didn't seem to bury their dead here, just prop them up on the verandahs.

In the parking lot of the general store, two old ladies watched from their rocking chairs as we got out of the truck. We went in. They followed. Annie took the left aisle. I took the right. The old ladies sought refuge behind the counter, not taking their eyes off us for a second. There were definitely strange vibes in the place. With the looks they were giving us, I wouldn't have been surprised to find our pictures pasted to a wall with the word "Wanted" underneath.

Finally, Annie located a bag of coffee. Great, we could get the hell out of there.

"Is that all?" grumbled one of the old ladies.

"Yes."

I took a few bills from my pocket and put them on the counter. The old lady unfolded them, pinning me with her eyes. Annie reminded me about the old man's package, but I hesitated; starting a conversation seemed like a quick way to end up with a shotgun pointing at my head.

"Oh, yes, I forgot," I began awkwardly, "Pierre-Paul Landry wanted me to see whether there was a package for him."

"You know Mr. Landry?"

"Well, yeah, we're spending a few days at his place."

The two old biddies sighed with relief, dangling smiles like wizened puppets.

"You'll have to forgive us for being a little wary. We saw you in his truck without him and we got suspicious. But if you know him, that changes everything. Are you family?"

"No, I work for him."

"Well, it's a pleasure. And you? Are you his girlfriend?"

"That's right. My name's Annie."

"Perhaps you have time for a drink?"

"We just finished breakfast."

"A little tipple helps the digestion."

"We're in a bit of a rush. We have an awful lot to do by tomorrow."

"You can't refuse. Mr. Landry himself started the tradition."

At last, something that didn't surprise me.

"Well, okay, but just a little one."

Our hostess filled four tiny glasses with a clear liquid from an unlabelled bottle. Then she and the other old lady threw back their drinks without so much as a grimace. Without hesitating, Annie did likewise. I drained my glass trustingly. The effect was interesting — like battery acid poured over a styrofoam stomach.

"It's my sister-in-law's special brew," the old lady told us, filling our glasses a second time.

"Delicious," I said, my vocal cords in shreds.

"Mr. Landry isn't sick, is he?" the other lady asked, setting down her thimble.

"No, not at all."

"We haven't seen much of him since his wife died."

"Horrible thing," the first lady continued. "He found her in the bathtub. She'd tripped and knocked her head."

"Then she drowned," the other felt the need to add. "It's just as well. She wasn't all there towards the end."

I couldn't help but think of the bathroom. I hoped he'd washed out the bathtub since. I knew it was ridiculous, but it was the first thing that came into my head. You just can't control that kind of thought.

"Mr. Landry told us she had Zeimer's disease," said the oldest old lady.

"Zeileimer's," the other one corrected her.

"What does it matter? She was crazy!"

"Don't say that, you're being mean."

"Okay, she wasn't crazy. She was sick in the head."

"Well, listen, if you'll both excuse us, we really should be on our way. If you could just give us Mr. Landry's package — if you've received it, of course."

"Why, certainly. Here it is," she said, taking out a very long box. "Be careful, it's pretty heavy."

•••

Annie took the wheel and got us back on the main road in no time, eyes fixed on the horizon and lips pressed tight together. Halfway between the village and the house, she stopped the truck on the shoulder. I knew I'd done something wrong. She turned to me slowly, her left eyelid twitching.

"Why didn't you tell me?"

"What?"

"That his wife was dead!"

"I don't know. I didn't see the point."

"The point is that I might have asked him certain questions that would have made him uncomfortable."

"I didn't think of that."

True enough, it was stupid. I just hadn't thought.

"You might try to think about something other than yourself, Julien."

At first my stomach was burning. Now it had spread to my brain.

"Men! You don't think about much besides your dicks."

It was our first real fight since we'd started seeing each other. Secretly, I thought it was kind of sweet.

"Living with a girl like you, it's hard to think about anything else."

Obviously I thought it was a compliment. Annie got out of the truck and slammed the door. I watched her walk away, hands in her pockets, shoulder blades moving under her T-shirt as the wind whipped her hair. I loved her so much it hurt, and I knew it was the kind of feeling that would lead me to the chopping block. It's impossible, you can't go through life like that; you have to protect yourself, barricade yourself behind something. But that's the paradox: when it hurts, you know you're not totally empty inside — there's still something left in your guts. Therein resides man's splendour, like a luminous crystal in the empty chamber of his heart. But us dumb-asses try to extinguish it. One day, goddamnit, we'll manage to put it out, and when that little flame is dead, we'll turn around, grief-stricken, and see that we never needed a nuclear bomb to destroy the planet, not when a simple lack of balls would do.

Anyway, as long as Annie was around, that wasn't going to happen to me. She was the dredger who snared me as I flailed at the bottom of the lake. She was the net that brought me back to the surface, the mouth that breathed air into my lungs. Annie was life.

I jumped behind the wheel and moved slowly down the road. The reassuring thing was that every time Annie left, she was already preparing her return. It would have scared me more if she stopped taking off. I slowed down more, adjusting my speed to hers, watching her with a beatific smile. That's what happens when beauty confronts you like divine grace.

"Sorry, Annie. You were right, I should've told you. I was insensitive."

"Is there anything else you want to tell me while we're at it?"

"Listen, we've only known each other for two months . . ."

"I like things to be clear so I don't trip over a bomb every time I turn a corner."

"Like you've told me everything? Come on, all I know about you is that you're twenty-five years old, you have a twenty-seven-day cycle, and you've fucked a cop."

She tried to hide a smile. Of course we all conceal things. If we had to reveal everything, we'd have a hard time making friends. For a first fight, I thought it ended pretty well. We were still novices in the area, and that was our strength; an old couple would have dragged it out for days.

The road was deserted, so I stopped the truck in the middle for a real kiss. Gusts of wind plastered her T-shirt against her chest, and I could clearly see her perfect, round breasts, and at the tip of each, an erect nipple defying the wind.

A few seconds later, the truck was on the shoulder with Annie and me sprawled over the front seat with our pants down around our ankles. A sunbeam was burning my left buttock, but that wasn't where it was the hottest. A little sunstroke was nothing compared to the stroking we had going.

Despite the intensity of the moment, the high pitch of excitement, her breasts that took turns in my mouth, her comforting cunt that welcomed me so warmly, and the gentle pelvic roll Annie added to my thrust — despite all that, I was thinking about the old man. It was true. I was thinking about Granddad, and about how hard it must have been to deal with it all — with his wife's death. He was a solid guy, but he talked so rarely it was impossible to know what was going on in his head, or how he'd brought himself out of mourning. I tried to derail that train of thought, because if Annie read my mind, I'd be a dead man.

"What do you think's in the package?" she asked, slightly out of breath.

"What?"

"What's in Granddad's package?" she repeated, opening her eyes.

"We fuck like rabbits out in the wilderness with the sun cooking our butts, and that's all you can come up with as love-talk?"

"Sorry, Julien. It was great — and I mean that — but I just can't help thinking about it."

I turned to look at the box. In the upper right corner, I noticed the word "Beretta" printed just beneath the drawing of a gun.

13

I woke up with Annie's underwear on my chest. Women develop all sorts of tricks to make us think of them. It looked like another gorgeous day. What I could see of the sky was entirely blue, except for a small tuft of shaving cream that someone hadn't wiped away.

"We're going," Annie announced, coming into the room.

"Where?"

"On a picnic," she answered, sitting on the bed. "Granddad knows a spot not far from here, so hurry up. I already made the coffee."

"We could take five minutes to get reacquainted."

She bounded off the bed just as I was about to grab her.

"Come on, get up! There's more to life than sex, Julien."

"You didn't always think so."

Before going out the door, she lifted her T-shirt and her

breasts gave me a candid look before disappearing behind their big cotton eyelid.

"We're leaving in ten minutes, with or without you."

I put on my jeans and grumbled into the kitchen, acknowledging no one. I swallowed down a cup of coffee left behind on the table. Cold coffee isn't so bad — only when you're not expecting it. With gym shoes in my left hand and T-shirt in my right, I went out of the house. It was the kind of day when a square metre of shade is worth a fortune on the black market. But I refused to be brought down by the heat.

I hopped into the truck and punched the horn three times. "Everyone stay calm. Women and old men first."

•••

The lake was the size of a football field and surrounded by trees. Exuberant, Annie looked everywhere at once, with a "shit!" here and a "super!" there. Granddad was proud of himself; his cavernous eyes were lit up like a couple of torches. I didn't say anything because I had nothing to say.

"Can we swim?" asked Annie.

"Do as you like, this is home. My father left it to me on the condition that I wouldn't build on it."

"That's a drag," I said.

"You could say that."

Annie undressed and galloped down to the lake. Some visions are definitely drawn directly from above. I swore I saw her breasts rise and fall in slow motion as they absorbed the momentum of her stride, and it made my knees weak. She jumped and shattered the watery mirror into a million pieces. What with the sunshine striking the surface at top speed, it was really something. Not as beautiful as a Volkswagen mirror, but not bad. I turned around, figuring that the old man would be riveted by the sight, but he was lying on the ground, the torches slowly flickering out.

"There's beer in the cooler," he mumbled.

As my experienced hand touched the cans, I suddenly felt the wind was about to change. I couldn't say why, but I knew something was up. I watched Annie making faces and I worried. I knew that equilibrium was a delicate thing, and that at any moment the waves could swamp the whole show. I put the top back on the cooler with the certainty that the gears had been set in motion and all the sand in the world couldn't stop them. In any case, we never have any say in it. The road is there and all we can do is get behind the wheel and follow it.

I went over to Granddad and handed him his can. We pulled the tabs almost simultaneously and our "pssiitts" echoed each other. I looked at him lying at my feet with the smile he kept for important occasions, and decided I was wrong to worry.

"She's a fine girl, that Annie."

"You didn't always think so."

"Being old doesn't take away your right to be stupid."

"True enough," I said, plopping my ass on the ground. "Annie's the best thing that ever happened to me."

"It's a good thing you see that. But you've got to watch it with her."

"Don't worry. She's the apple of my eye. I keep her in my sights."

"In that case, what are you waiting for? Go join her."

It was that simple: if I put my big toe in the lake, I'd be

committing my whole foot to the workings of fate. As long as I did nothing, there was a chance everything could remain the same. But the minute I agreed to join the damned game, I knew the whole thing would unfold at incredible speed.

"I will. Soon enough," I told the old man. "You have to let the desire mount inside you, you have to really want it, otherwise you just shiver to death."

He looked at me skeptically. I smiled broadly, with the arrogance of youth. He lifted his can. A well-intentioned toast, a toast that all the ill will in the world couldn't hold back. Our cans knocked as a handful of spray rose up in the air.

Annie was waving her arms in my direction. I envied the fish swimming around her. There are some curves that water can't distort.

"Julien! Come on!"

It's not out of lack of desire, my pretty one.

"The water's great!"

No way to fight against it. I felt like a pawn taken by surprise by a crazed bishop. I had to move — I had no choice. Anyway, what could possibly happen to us? As long as we were together, we'd have some kind of shelter, wouldn't we?

I pulled off my T-shirt and walked towards the lake. My jeans and underwear ended up on a big rock. The water was cold enough to get the blood going without freezing it. I immersed myself slowly, trying to remember how you were supposed to coordinate your arms and legs so you didn't end up on the bottom.

"It's great, isn't it? Come closer."

"That's what I'm trying to do, Annie."

I swam as far as I could, until I was able to put my hands on her shoulders. Two lifesavers jutted against my chest, awakening instincts that never slept very soundly, as you've probably noticed by now.

She broke free and swam towards the middle of the lake. I watched her, not forgetting to keep up the piston motion with my legs. Scientists claim that the human body is seventy-eight percent water. If that's the case, why do we have so much trouble keeping our heads above its surface?

Annie broke off and turned back towards me.

"You coming?"

"Depends on where we're going."

"The destination's not important."

How can anyone say such a thing? How can we think it's not important, considering what's hanging in the air, considering what the little waves in the parallel world are cooking up for us? That's the kind of ignorance that'll send us into the next world.

She waited for me a couple of strokes, then raced ahead. It looked like we were really going to swim the lake. No matter — my love is swimming, so I am too. Servitude is a wonderful thing.

I finally ended up on a beach. Annie was already lying on the sand. Propped up on her elbows, she was watching the sun on her belly. I covered the last few metres on all fours, short of breath, my side shot through by a terrific cramp. She watched me crumple at her side.

"Feels good, doesn't it?"

"Sure, if you think that feeling good requires pain."

"Listen, Julien, I have something to tell you. I've been mulling it over for a while, but I guess I've been putting off talking about it. Finally, just now, I decided that if I can't tell you, there's no sense spending our lives together. Understand? If we can't share everything, we're better off not being together. You follow?"

A burning sun in a clear blue sky wasn't that much different from hell after all. "Not really, but go on anyway."

"Okay, but I want you to listen to everything I have to say. Take the time to think before you answer, okay?"

"I can do that for you. Go ahead."

"I want to have a baby."

"I'm sure if we look hard enough, we'll find one somewhere."

"I'm serious, Julien. I want us to have a kid together."

At times like this, I always think to look for the hidden cameras.

"We'd be so happy with a little girl or a little boy. Watching him grow up, showing him stuff, helping him discover life, you know?"

You'd have to be blind not to see the currents swirling inside her. The kind of currents that swell into undertows and smash into cliffs. The kind that can destroy everything. A huge wave of love isn't far from a tidal wave.

"It's not as simple as all that, Annie. We've got no money and no car, we've only known each other for two months, and we have no idea what's going to happen to us."

If we continued this way, nothing would ever happen to us. Separately, maybe, but not together. She shook her head and took a deep breath as her breasts pointed savagely towards the sky.

"Those are men's excuses. Two months or two years, what difference does it make? If it's going to work, it'll work. If it's going to end, it'll end. Time changes nothing. I want a baby, and that's that. We don't have to do it right away. I just want you to think about it."

"Life's like matches — you shouldn't play with it. When you decide to light one, whether you're lighting a cigarette or setting something on fire, you have to know what the damned flame is supposed to do."

The image of her little belly all swollen up was so real to me that the hairs on my arms stood up.

"Anyway, why do you want . . . *that*?"

"What a question! You don't ask a woman why she wants to have a baby. She wants one, that's all. Any old guy could give her one. I just want it to be you."

"Thank you."

"Don't be stupid."

"I'm not, I like that you've chosen me."

I tried everything, but I knew I'd lost her. Again I looked at her body in the sun. She was so luminous you had to wonder who was lighting up who. Suddenly the brightness moved and stretched and unfolded and achieved the vertical position. She was standing, splitting the wind like the mast of a schooner, while I lay on the ground at her feet, totally knocked out.

"Now's not a good time, anyway. That's all I can say at the moment. But I don't want things to change between us," I tried.

She thought that over for a second. I knew she appreciated my intentions, but I wasn't sure they were enough. She took a few steps towards the water and waded slowly into it. When she was in up to her thighs, she turned and looked at me carefully. At first, there was a need to know in her eyes, then curiosity changed to condemnation. I could read all the bitterness in the world, all its disillusionment in her expression.

"Fuck off, shithead!"

I had no answer. I knew my small fists would bounce off her belly of marble. Sadly, I watched that ass, marked by the curse, disappear beneath the waves. For the first time, I watched with total disinterest.

PART 3

14

Strange weather. As if the old man had packed up all the cold fronts in the region and put them in his suitcase. Mind you, Africa can swallow up all the north winds she wants to; if elephants flap their ears there, it's certainly not to keep them warm. Anyway, for the time being, we had nothing to complain about. Here it was, December 22, and there wasn't more than two centimetres of snow on the ground. In town, I supposed, it wasn't even cold enough to keep the dog turds frozen.

If that was Granddad's dream, what could we do about it? I said to him, "The place isn't for you. Mosquitoes wanting to suck your blood, snakes wrapping themselves around your neck like wreaths, and all those creatures quietly sleeping in the jungle while you, like a murderer's apprentice, land in the middle of their peaceful paradise with the force of an atom bomb. It's completely insane." That's what I told him, but he didn't listen. He wanted to be right instead.

On the other hand, Annie did have a good point. A change of scene might do him good. I gave in. Granddad, I give you my blessing, go in peace, we'll look after everything. He gave me a big kiss on the cheek. He didn't smell like alcohol since he hadn't gotten on the plane yet — he intended on staying sober for his first flight. I kept my mouth closed, but I figured that, what with the supply he'd already taken on during his career, sobriety the way we meant it was pretty well meaningless.

When the time came, he went off with his little suitcase, his oversized pants, and his senior citizen status. That's what death is, I thought: you leave with a tenth of the things you accumulated during your miserable life, and even though you thought you knew it all, it's like trying to ride a bike for the first time. Except that, when death's involved, no one's there to run alongside in case you chicken out. So long, Granddad, come back in one piece with a set of chimpanzee antlers for the den.

I sat down in the living room to enjoy the crap that had been printed in last week's newspaper. Meanwhile, Annie was upstairs, practising her prenatal exercises.

I thought I was doing the right thing, telling Granddad I'd look after Dalida the cow, but, honestly, I was beginning to count the days. I missed the paranoids stalking the subway corridors, the skinheads who'd smash anybody's face in for the sheer pleasure of it, and the kindergarten kids who played with the condoms and needles they happened to find in the playground. Ah, the city! The real, live city! With its inmates running the asylum, its trigger-happy cops, its burned-out youth.

Annie came hurtling down the staircase, shouting that a car was coming.

"A car?"

"Yeah, a car? You know what that is?"

You have to understand that here, during the winter, and the summer, too, no one comes to visit. The last car anyone saw around here belonged to a guy who missed his turn-off in the late fifties. So, when absolutely nothing happens for decades, a car showing up is like a fruit stand that's sprouted overnight in the Sahara Desert.

I forgot about the jumble of lies I was reading and stood next to Annie at the window. I put my arm around her waist. We looked like an old farm couple waiting for their son to return from the war.

The car pulled up by the truck. We glanced at each other; we didn't recognize it. I had no trouble identifying the human figures, however. Some shapes you see once in your life and never forget them. I opened the door.

"What are you doing here?"

Sonia smiled and offered a pair of cheeks barely reddened by the cold. I kissed her. Pierrot offered his hand, and I shook it heartily. I made the usual introductions since they didn't know Annie. Other cheeks were offered, other lips alit there, then all of us looked at each other, not too sure what to say next.

"You bought a new car," I said, for lack of a better subject.

"A Mustang convertible."

"Wow!"

"It's just an old 1966," Sonia informed us. "I had to rebuild the engine."

Some girls can smash a stereotype to smithereens, just

that quick. Which made me think that she and Annie might get along fine. They both had a way of storming into the temple, scattering the money-lenders, and turning over the tables, then setting up shop themselves like representatives of truth from on high. We'd all benefit from a change of pace. Especially Annie. After all, I was just an ordinary guy, and with ordinary guys, everything gets pretty ordinary pretty fast.

"I was wondering where you'd gone to," Pierrot explained. "I kept calling, but the phone was cut off."

"Then we stopped by your place," Sonia added, pressing against him. "There were two tons of junk mail in your mailbox."

"Yeah? Well, we've been here for a while."

"Then we went to the market. All I had to do was ask one question and I got all the details — including the address."

"If I'd known you were coming, I would have asked you to stay a few days."

A wide grin spread across Pierrot's face. The kind of suspicious-looking rictus you see on vacuum-cleaner salesmen's faces as they leave some gullible person's house. His little squinting, moist, luminous eyes slid slowly in Sonia's direction, then cut back to me.

"Our stuff is in the car."

Sonia and Annie went to get their grip in T-shirts and shoes. I ushered Pierrot into the living room and took a good look at him.

"It's been a hell of a long time."

"Yeah."

"You two still couple of the year?"

"Couldn't be better. You were right, Julien. I think this time she's the one."

"I'm happy for you."

We smiled like a pair of nuns, and if we were just a little stupider, we would have given each other a big hug.

"Maybe you don't know, but Bill and Paule are expecting us on the first of January. You can come with Annie. It's for New Year's Day, of course, but it's a party for Paule, too."

"It's not her birthday."

"No, but she's pregnant."

"Oh, no!"

Just then the girls came back with bags in their hands. They dropped them in the kitchen and went outside again.

"How's Bill handling it?"

"Pretty good. He repainted the whole apartment, with one room half blue, half pink. He wants to avoid stereotypes."

"Don't mention it to Annie, okay? I'll tell you why later."

"Does she want you to repaint her apartment?"

"Later," I told him as the girls came in with bags of groceries.

A good atmosphere seemed to have settled in. It was great — I didn't ask why, I took it like a gift from above. I was as happy as a clam at high tide, and I didn't stop to think that good atmospheres can suddenly turn very dangerous.

We popped a top as Sonia told us how she'd moved on to painting. She was doing street portraiture, following Pierrot's advice. It was dull as dust but it paid a hundred times better than forty hours a week in the needle trade. As we popped another top, Pierrot described how he intended to help Sonia make a name for herself in the world of fashion design. I opened another one and tried to understand how this poor girl was going to draw portraits in the street all day, then go home at night and design a line of clothing. Finally, I got tired of opening beer cans and got out the bottle of Scotch.

We slid gently into a fuzzy coma. With Pierrot, Sonia, and Annie around, the night was like a steaming-hot shower on a winter morning. I'd just about stopped talking, listening with a bemused ear and a ridiculous smile on my face. I pictured Granddad, riding on the back of a mammoth, a Beretta in his hand under the African sun, then I buzzed back to the living room again, sipping a bit of peace from everyone's expression.

When we finally made it upstairs to bed, I found myself lying on my back, eyes wide open, unable to sleep. It was a big moment; I had the three most important people in my life with me. Three big slices that could turn this joint into a kind of gigantic celestial elevator, leaving this poor earth behind and reaching heavenward, scattering wide fluorescent waves. As you can imagine, I was also pretty smashed.

Take Annie, for example. It's amazing what we'd gone through in the last six months. The girl had done me a world of good. I wasn't the guy I used to be. For example, when Pierrot showed up, I didn't start crying, I didn't hang onto his leg like a dying man. I kept cool, I took one mouthful after another, nice and easy, to keep from choking. She'd helped me in a lot of other ways, too. Actually, this business about having a kid was the only thing messing up my mind. But, what the hell, every girl on earth carries her own El Dorado — and her own Vietnam.

Honestly, were those prenatal exercises really necessary?

All right, maybe they are useful, but only for certain kinds of women. Pregnant ones, for example. Which was definitely not her case. Since the incident at the lake, I'd invented one subterfuge after another to keep one of my timid spermatozoa from reaching her predatory egg. I must have been the envy of all the guys, since I'd become a premature ejaculator by *choice*. So fast am I, gentlemen, that when I'm at my best, I can reach climax *before* penetration. That's just how good I'd gotten.

The process wasn't difficult: as soon as Annie brought up the subject of carnal relations, I screened an outrageous sequence of hyper-pornographic images in my own private theatre. Obviously, I couldn't keep the game going indefinitely; she sulked and pouted and looked offended. Next, I learned to pull out just before the crucial moment. It's hard to explain that to your partner; I had to express my regrets and make up some nonsense about the last thrust being hard to control for a man. That lasted three weeks.

Then I was afflicted by a painful right testicle for ten days or so, after which Granddad announced that he was going on a safari, and all the preparations and adjustments created stress that prevented me from achieving an erection. Annie started to say that, sexually, I was the most complicated guy she'd ever met. I took that as a compliment. But she saw through me pretty quickly. She got so pissed off she wouldn't let me touch her for a good three weeks. At first I was relieved, though after that regimen, I started to suffer from violent pains in a certain gland. When a woman of Annie's calibre walks around naked in front of you, you start realizing that more than your brain possesses the gift of memory. After a few days, hell took the elevator and got off at my floor.

Things went back to normal. More or less. Annie finally let us use condoms; only thing was, she started doing those infernal exercises every day. She figured she'd wear me down, but I have worked up a tolerance. Life can't do much about a guy like me. Its despotic assaults strike me full in the chest, only to roll off like marshmallows. But I wasn't exactly lighthearted, which was why I was happy to see Pierrot. We all needed a change of pace.

I got dressed and went out for a little fresh air. Sonia was sitting on the porch railing.

"Can't you sleep?" I asked her.

"No."

"I know what it's like. It comes and goes. Sleep is a mysterious thing."

"I guess . . ."

She and I never had it easy. Pierrot often put us in difficult situations, but I thought we worked our way out pretty well.

"Is something bothering you?"

"Yes. Julien, I'm in trouble."

Of course she was. I must have the kind of face that makes people want to confess. Come to me, little children, and with my toilet-paper soul I'll wipe your shitty little problems clean.

"I'm listening."

"I'm pregnant."

What's the matter with all of them? Instead of grabbing her by the throat and squeezing until I heard something snap, I managed to stammer out something, anything, even if I didn't believe a word of it.

"That's nice."

"Actually, it's not."

Just what I figured. I tried to get through to the fundamental issue. That's all that matters: life is a sprint, and if you want to make the cut, you can't lose a second.

"Does Pierrot know?"

"That's the complication," she told me.

"Did you tell him?"

"No."

"Do you mind me asking what you're waiting for?"

"I wanted to know what you think."

"Do you mind me asking what I have to do with it?" As you can see, I didn't have my kid gloves on.

"I don't know, I thought you were the kind of guy that a woman could talk things over with."

I sealed my lips to keep the avalanche of bitter commentary from pouring out.

"Do you get the picture?" she asked.

"That's the problem: I don't. I don't know why all of you come running to me when your uterus is involved. I don't understand what women think — okay? Whatever that thing you've got inside is, no doubt it's infinitely beautiful, but sometimes it's just a pain in the ass."

I stopped there; I didn't know how much further I'd go if I kept up. The great December silence settled over our pinheads. With the numbing effect of alcohol and the cold, a black screen began closing over my eyes. Sonia tore that screen apart by getting up and standing right in front of me. A tear sparkled in the night.

"I thought you could help me."

A crying woman is a majestic thing; it's also very dangerous. It's a mantrap, a crevasse at your feet that'll swallow you up at the first false move. I took her in my arms and closed my eyes to blot out the dizziness. I held her with all the strength I had left. You never know: maybe the whole business would dry up and blow away, maybe the great nightmare of life would come to an abrupt end and we'd all wake up in a fancy Jamaican beach house with coconut palms, rum, and a reggae band.

"Listen, Sonia, it can't be such a disaster. Pierrot's not an asshole, he'll understand. Together, you'll find a solution. Nothing's impossible when you're young and have the faith."

I knew I was talking nonsense, but you can never lay it on too thick.

"You don't understand, Julien."

"I know."

"Pierrot isn't the father — that's the problem."

At first I felt relieved for him. Then I realized that what had seemed like a simple change of plans was actually a monumental tragedy. It's fascinating that creatures as tiny as spermatozoa can cause so much uproar.

"Do you realize the mess you're in?"

"Yes," she admitted, depositing another tear on her left cheek.

"Don't say anything to Pierrot. Anyway, how can you be sure it's not his?"

"At the end of November, we decided not to see each other for a couple of weeks, to have a little time to think it over . . ."

"That must not have been Pierrot's idea."

"No, it was mine. I met another guy. Just for one night. I was feeling down, he cheered me up, we got carried away — that's how it happened."

I felt like telling her that such a thing could never happen with me since I'd mastered the withdrawal technique, but I figured this wasn't the moment. I looked for something else to say, but the results weren't brilliant.

"You're in deep shit, Sonia," I told her.

"Thanks, but I already knew that."

"Pierrot doesn't know you were with another guy?"

"No. And I think he'd take the news pretty hard."

"That's not the half of it," I said to myself softly.

"What was that?"

"Nothing."

"Maybe if I talked it over with Annie . . ."

"No, don't do that!"

"What should I do? You know Pierrot better than I do."

"Let me think about it."

"How much time do you need?"

"A few days, okay?"

"All right. Thank you, Julien."

"Go inside now. You don't want your embryo catching cold."

I figured that was the kind of thing women like to hear — a small confirmation of their fertility. I may not understand everything, but I'm not completely insensitive. Certainly not insensitive to the rising tide, and the load of shit riding it. I decided to go back to Annie. There's no refuge like a siren's body when the sea begins throwing up some death-dealing waves. Not that I felt like fucking — no, I just wanted to close my eyes and sleep forever.

I pulled the blankets over us and curled up against her in the total blackness of the room.

"Is that you?" she sighed.

"No, it's him."

"Can't you sleep?"

"I'm all right."

She took my hand, which I'd placed on her side, and put it over her heart loosely.

"I've got a funny feeling, Julien."

"What's that?"

"You're going to say I've got a one-track mind."

"Nothing surprises me anymore."

"Sonia's pregnant."

"*What?* What makes you say that?"

"I just feel it. Details never lie."

"I didn't notice anything," I said.

"It's the kind of thing only a woman can see."

Voilà, another territory with a No Trespassing sign on it, another fence separating us from the wonderful world of woman's intuition.

"What do you think?"

"Nothing!"

"You think I'm wrong?"

"No. But I do think you're all going to drive us crazy one of these days."

"There are some things you just refuse to see."

"Yes. And I'm glad of it."

15

A few flakes had floated down overnight. The sky was as grey as a bad dream, the wind as cutting as death, and as I did my best to shovel, I was struck by the certainty that life was shit.

This morning I had been treated to the sight of Sonia in a kimono, kicking the shit out of a hundred imaginary enemies as the smell of fresh coffee spread through the house. I tried to spot the telltale sign of the swelling belly, but no dice.

Pierrot woke up as usual — when breakfast was on the table — and dragged himself down to the kitchen, half-naked, since he can't get dressed until he's had his second cup of coffee. He hadn't slept so well in years; according to him, it was due to the country air. I suggested that he go to hell: alcohol was the real culprit. My nerves were buzzing like bees and someone was banging a tambourine in my skull. I hadn't slept for more than an hour.

Later, Sonia used a moment of shared solitude to ask if I'd thought it over. I told her no, then dropped my toast and peanut butter on my plate, put on my coat, and sauntered out into the snowy immensity of the morning.

As my nose sent out dual cones of condensation, I thought of all those uteruses, and every shovelful required a superhuman effort. Fortunately, Pierrot pitched in with another shovel. I felt a sense of relief as fresh blood began to feed my muscles. As long as Pierrot was nearby, Sonia wouldn't harass me. Without trying to, we fell into rhythm together. Besides Siamese twins, no one lives in such symbiosis. I couldn't tell you why; it's just one of those great mysteries involving waves, humours, and fundamental rhythms.

"Things all right with Sonia?" I asked casually.

"Yes."

"You're travelling hand in hand down the great path to happiness?"

"If you want to put it that way."

"You know you can trust me, Pierrot."

"I've got nothing to say."

"Sure?"

"Uh-huh."

"That's what I'm here for . . ."

"I know that."

"Don't hold back," I said, leaning on my shovel. "You can tell me if there's something bothering you."

"Okay. Now that you've made me feel completely comfortable, there is something I'd like to tell you."

"Yes?"

"Your questions bug the hell out of me."

I sunk my shovel into the snow. Seeing that I was completely absorbed by the job, Pierrot attacked. I was blinded by a giant white sheet that exploded in my face. Not about to let myself be buried, I showed that young asshole how it was done. I put half the snow down his jacket and he really got mad. At that point I decided to head for the house. Which was unfortunate for Annie and Sophie, who were having a quiet conversation over a cup of coffee — that is, until Pierrot charged in with his hands full of snow. He launched it in my direction, but the girls got the worst of it. After a few cries of protest, Annie ran outside to stock up on ammunition, while Sonia knocked Pierrot to the floor. Annie came back and shoved half her snow harvest in each one of his ears.

Not yet satisfied, the girls teamed up to tickle him to death, one concentrating on his belly, the other on his armpits. I watched the show and said to myself that there was nothing finer than a human being forgetting his troubles and rolling around on all fours with his paws in the air. A dog taught me that. Then I thought of Annie going nuts over me giving her a kid, and Pierrot who was going to kill himself when he found out *he* was going to have one, and it all started whirling faster and faster, all this bullshit that women put us through, and how we're never up to it, how we spend our lives saying *excuse me* because we got carried away, but we get carried away because we're never up to it, but if we're not up to it, maybe it's because their demands are completely out of touch with reality. Which proves that love isn't possible, it doesn't exist; it's just another idol we invented to avoid dying in pain and solitude, to avoid admitting that we're bloodthirsty murderers hunting down good red meat, lusting for a good fuck for its own sake on a hilltop under the moon while a few kilometres away, the wolves howl out their voracious hunger because they never invented idols for themselves. At that point I thought I'd better get some fresh air before it got too late.

Outside, I had a terrible realization: *there was snow down my back!* I pulled my T-shirt from my pants and tried to free myself from the enemy's embrace.

"What are you doing?" asked Annie, from behind me.

"Nothing."

"Can't we have a little fun anymore?"

"Sure, we can. In fact, that's all we can do."

"What's the matter now?"

"Nothing."

"In a good mood as usual!"

See, you're never up to their level.

Pierrot appeared. "What's up?"

"Nothing!"

"I've seen you in better shape, Julien."

"We all have our moments."

"Sure. But we're here to have a good time, have a few laughs."

"I get the picture. Too bad we don't have a special button to push and automatically relax when the time comes."

"What's bugging you?" he asked, pulling his cigarettes out of his coat pocket.

"It's complicated, Pierrot."

Of course, just then, Sonia arrived, and if you ask me, she looked awfully worried.

"What's going on? Is something wrong?"

"Everything's perfect," I told her.

"What would you think," she chimed in, "if instead of looking for each other's faults, we got together and made a really big Christmas dinner?"

I stood there a second or two. Amazing, I'd completely forgotten about the holidays. Mind you, Christmas has never done much for me. But I was game to try it one more time, at the risk of getting caught up in the Yuletide spirit, as they call it.

"Oh, great!" Annie exclaimed, squeezing Sonia with all her might.

"Why not?" Pierrot said. "We can get some good food, blow some money on really good wine, and spend all day tomorrow making dinner."

"Oh, great!" Annie exclaimed, squeezing Pierrot with all her might.

"Why not?" I said, jumping on the bandwagon. "We can take this afternoon to look for presents for each other."

"Oh, great!" Annie exclaimed, covering my face with kisses.

In two seconds we had pumped ourselves up, each with his or her own personal vision of the evening, and it was obvious that in everyone's mind, everything was smooth as silk. Especially in Sonia's. She wanted a few minutes to forget that little ball of flesh growing in her belly. In other words, everything was better than perfect, we'd hit nirvana — life was a waking dream. Pretty soon, with the wisdom of hindsight, I'd come to see that's how the devil managed to sell us a few acres of hell, but for the time being, everything seemed so harmless.

16

Pierrot volunteered to hang garlands around the doors and windows. I held the materials for him and made sure to open the beers at the right moment. In between Christmas carols that he happily parodied, he kept bellowing that these knickknacks were really cheap shit, that they shouldn't even exist, that it was highway robbery to sell that kind of crap, and what about Rudolph the red-nosed reindeer, wasn't he the cutest little thing, with his shiny red nose and his spotted red dick — you would even say it glowed.

The girls would show up any minute now. They had set out at dawn because they absolutely wanted to take the stores by surprise. We took care of that yesterday; today, we looked after the decorations, and, let me tell you, we spared no effort. You should have seen the table and the kitchen chairs: it took three hours, two rolls of tape, and sixty Christmas lights, but the effect was extraordinary. The kitchen wasn't the right place, so we carried it all up to the upstairs room. We pushed the bed aside and put the table near the window, facing the fireplace. We'd show those women — even if we were only men, we could still have a romantic thought from time to time.

We were enjoying a quiet end to the afternoon. Everything was looking up and spirits were high. A solid good mood, so solid it felt like the day was made of poured concrete. Everything would be fine. When I had opened my eyes that morning, I promised myself to forget all the swords of Damocles hanging over our heads. Of course, it was easier said than done, but I'd just about made it. It was like asking a guy who's had a leg amputated to think about the one he has left. I'd just about made it.

I went down to the kitchen. You have to be careful with rabbit. As often as possible, you have to take him by the head and the thighs and turn him over. The rabbit had been in there for twenty-three hours now; he looked like he was bursting with wine. I took him out of the fridge. He hadn't moved; he was still lying on his side with his little feet all stretched out. Any fresher than that, he'd have to be alive. We picked him up yesterday afternoon not far from here. The guy told us to choose one and he practically skinned it right before our eyes. At the time I was pretty disgusted, but what can you do, we're carnivores, why try to hide it? After all, even if he hadn't lived much over twelve months, I was sure he'd copulated more often than I had in twenty-six years. We're born to die; we might as well be prepared to pay our debt.

While we were at it, we picked up a few quails. Annie knew a good recipe that involved seedless green grapes. I was into rabbit — I was born with it, marinated rabbit flows in my veins, there's nothing I can do about it. The first time I laid my hands on one, I knew right away I was going to create a work of genius. There's no explanation, it was beyond words, a kind of telepathic link-up between the victim and the perpetrator. Those poor little animals speak to me when they reach their peak. So, tonight, considering the great shape I was in, I felt confident that this little wonder would knock us out of our seats.

I looked out the window, impatient for the girls to be back. I pictured all of us, busy as bees, fixing the last details so everything would be perfect as the smell of rabbit rose up to the second floor and mingled with the scent of maple wood quietly crackling in the fireplace. I don't know why, but I prefer the preparations to the actual celebration. Everyone works on his little part, and then it all comes together in the end. You drop what you're doing for a minute and see what the others are up to, you congratulate each other, you get all excited, you steal a quick kiss if you happen to run into your baby by the fridge, then you return to your business, alone and lost in concentration, like madmen building an Eiffel Tower out of matchsticks.

Next we moved onto the tree. Okay, so we didn't go out and cut down a tree in the forest — there isn't any forest here. But we did use the ceiling to fasten a large triangle of garlands, which we then lashed to the floor. I placed three presents underneath; Pierrot did the same. The results of yesterday's shopping. We bought everything together, except for the gift we would give each other, of course. The wrapping was magnificent, full of pastel colours, silky little ribbons, and words of love on flowery cards. With women, you can't afford to forget that part. They don't care about the price of the gift, it means nothing to them. It's easy to take money out of your pocket and lay it on the counter. It takes more time to put together a nice presentation. That's how they decide on how interested you are in them. To make sure we didn't blow it, we put our money on the counter and the official wrapper-upper made us a nice package.

The Mustang came up the gravel road. Everything was perfect, immaculate, there wasn't a hair out of place. The girls came in, their arms loaded with bags, yelling and laughing like lumberjacks. They gave us quick pecks on the cheek, nothing too generous.

"What did you do with the table?" Sonia asked.

"We put it upstairs."

"Oh, I want to see it," Annie begged.

"No, not until everything's ready."

I put the bag of presents by the stairway, and one glance, as quick as it was subtle, told me there were six gifts, one of which was very small and inoffensive. The biggest surprises sometimes come in the smallest packages.

Pierrot was a lot more interested in the bottle bag. His hand dove into it like a guy with a foot fetish who's just gotten a job in a high-heel shoe factory.

"A Chablis!" he quivered, biting on his lower lip. "Mark my words, Julien, when it comes to dry white wine, there's nothing better."

"That's nice," I said absently.

"What? A Maréchal Foch?" he grunted as he pulled out a second bottle.

"While I was at it," Sonia interrupted him, "I got two

Médocs and two Saint-Emilions."

"Wow!"

I slipped in behind him, just in case he fainted. But he kept his feet on solid ground, holding one bottle up to the light, reading the other one's label, commenting on the year. I took a 1996 out of the fridge, noted the fine colour and the perfect temperature, unscrewed the cap, and poured half the contents down my throat before letting loose with a mighty belch.

•••

According to my instinct, without having to resort to a fork or any other instrument, I knew that in sixteen minutes the rabbit would be perfect. I took the quails out of the oven and gently pushed the door closed, sending a kiss through the little window. The girls were in the living room, so keyed up they couldn't sit still. I placed the little birdies on their plates with parsley sprigs all around. The girls watched me climb the stairs with supplicant eyes, the way a desert might gaze at a raincloud.

I took a last look around to make sure everything was perfect. The bottle of white wine was reposing on ice on the mantelpiece, the fire was burning nicely, it was exactly nine-thirty, a few fluffy flakes were beginning to fall. I stuck the plug in the outlet and the table was illuminated. I looked at Pierrot solemnly. Everything was perfect; I must have been dreaming. We sat down so we could see the stairway.

"Okay, you can come up now!"

"Yeah!" they cried in unison.

"Slowly, now!"

We heard them take the first few steps. The usual groaning of the stairway mingled with the sound of the crackling fire. The top of their hair appeared simultaneously. They took another step, then we saw their eyes grow wide and their expressions freeze in a mixture of pleasure and amazement. They were like two little girls who had been awakened for a midnight supper. We'd really succeeded this time.

"It's great!" Annie exclaimed as she bounded up the last few stairs.

"You guys are crazy," Sonia added. "How long did it take you to put all that together?"

Annie circled the celestial table, one hand trailing over the tablecloth and the backs of the chairs.

"It looks like a flying saucer."

Coming from Annie, that means something. She knows about such things; apparently you can see a lot of them on her native planet. I knew we'd made our mark by the looks on their faces. Now that our ship was under way, we'd have them in our thrall all night. They were ours now: we'd spring one surprise after another on them, from one big gun to the next until they couldn't take it anymore, until they asked for a time out, until they begged for a moment's respite. And that's when we'd finish them off with our respective little guns. *Vulgarium jokus.*

We uncorked the bottles, massacred the quails, devoured the rabbit, delicately, of course, so as not to disturb its tender flesh, all accompanied by, "Wow, Julien, I never ate anything this good," and "I don't know how you do it, man," and "Julien, where did you learn to make rabbit that way?"

"Cooks *learn* to make rabbit," I explained, "but artists are born with it."

We uncorked more bottles as the mercury kept climbing, inside as well as outside. Pierrot was looking after the fire and, as usual, he didn't know when to stop. It was fabulous at first, the flames were snapping and crackling like fireworks, the heat flowed over us in waves, it crept up our spines and necks until it swaddled our heads, and it felt great. A great numbing wave of heat from without; meanwhile, the wine took care of the numbness from within. We weren't paying attention to anything, we were too busy cackling like crows in between bites and sips, but after a while, it became unbearable.

"Do you mind if I open the window a little?"

"Go ahead, Julien, we could use some air."

We sure could; we were all soaked to the skin. I opened the window ever so slightly and an army of snowflakes invaded the room, riding a south wind that augured no good. I closed the window again. You couldn't see to the end of your arm out there. The flakes were as big as pieces of popcorn and as wet as does' eyes.

"When do we open the presents?"

"At midnight, Annie, that's the twentieth time we've told you. Relax. Do you want another piece of cake?"

"No. But I would like to know what time it is."

"It's . . . just a second," said Pierrot, searching for his watch that lay deep in his pocket. "It's five minutes past midnight."

"Already?" I asked.

"I can tell time. It's five minutes past midnight."

"I knew we'd miss it," Annie sighed.

"Are you sure your watch is right?"

"Sure, I'm sure," he said, popping the cork on a

Saint-Emilion. "By now, the Virgin Mary must be changing her first diaper."

The girls laughed but I said nothing. I stared at the puddle of leftover cream in my plate. There it was: the great wheel had turned. That's why everything was slowly fading out. We were entering a period of transition. Suddenly, it was too hot in the room, a white Christmas had turned into a drizzly one and midnight had slipped by without anyone noticing.

"Don't drink the Saint-Emilion," Pierrot grimaced. "It's gone vinegary."

If that wasn't proof that the great beam of happiness had begun to sag, then I don't know what was.

"A bottle of vinegary wine isn't going to stop us," Pierrot declared. "There's plenty more where that came from."

Poor suckers, put your hands over your eyes and pretend you don't see the obvious.

"Well, if that's the case," Sonia proposed, "what are we waiting for? Let's open the presents!"

"Oh, yes!" Annie cried.

Finally, someone had a good idea. Maybe the presents would get us back on track. Though, considering the suggestion came from Sonia, I'd be inclined to expect the worst.

"All right," I agreed, "what are we waiting for? Let's not let any crap get in our way."

"That's right. There's lots of boxes just dying to be opened."

"Okay, Annie, you hand them around."

"All right," she agreed, standing on her chair. "But first, since I'm so hot, I'm going to take off my shirt."

"All right!!"

She sent the piece of fabric flying onto the bed, and we all stood gaping a second at the black camisole that attempted to conceal her breasts. That gave the troops a real pick-me-up. We got ahold of ourselves, shook off our doldrums, emptied our glasses, put the Saint-Emilion aside, and opened a Médoc instead.

"Where do I start?"

"Give my present to Julien," Sonia said.

"Your wish is my command."

Annie moved in on me, package in hand, but my attention was mainly on what was swinging and swaying beneath her flimsy camisole.

"To Julien, from Sonia," she announced, kissing me on the ear.

"It's not much, but we did agree on a ten-dollar limit. But before you open it, I want you to know that I got it for you because of what Annie told me."

I tore open the paper. Inside was a small box covered with Chinese characters. I opened it and discovered a vial with more characters on it.

"Thank you, it's very nice. But what is it?"

They could hardly suppress their laughter.

"What is it?"

"Well, you take a little spoonful . . ."

"Yes?"

"And it gives you a hard-on! Ha, ha, ha!"

I should have known my sexual non-exploits would come back to haunt me. General euphoria broke out. They were all slapping their thighs, gasping for breath, practically choking, then bursting out in howls of laughter again.

"Okay, who's next?" I asked, my heart filled with vengeance.

"Pierrot!"

"Yes, we want Pierrot! We want Pierrot!" Pierrot chanted.

His was a pretty little package wrapped in red paper. Cute as anything, with Annie's name on it. He opened it slowly and discovered a pair of underwear with a candy cane printed on it. A single cane. I don't have to tell you where they put it, those dirty-minded people. And I think I'll skip the obscenities that were bandied about as they split their sides with laughter. It was quite a spectacle, a pair of scarlet-faced women wallowing in triviality.

Then came Annie's turn. Pierrot insisted she open his gift. The box was big; its contents, light. The girls probably figured we were going to give them a dose of their own medicine, but we'd had romantic thoughts on our mind, and the presents we bought showed it. For once, man — that barbarous, crude beast — took the trouble to try a little tenderness, whereas woman, that subtle, delicate little jewel, sank into absolute vileness. No doubt there was some lesson to be learned from that sociological nose-thumbing.

"Wow!" Annie exclaimed, dropping the box on the floor, "it's super-beautiful!"

She took out the ring from its little case and examined it from all angles.

"We said ten dollars at most."

"I got it at a discount."

Discount, my eye. I was there when he slipped it under his jacket.

"It says ten karats!"

"Quite a sale," Sonia snapped. "You're the only one who can find discounts like that."

"You know me, I've always been lucky with bargains."

"I don't know if luck is the word for it," she said.

Annie was completely deaf to the proceedings. Wide-eyed, she tried the ring on each of her fingers.

"Why don't we give Sonia her present?" Pierrot suggested.

"Julien," Annie told me, "give her the little box, right there, on the floor. It comes from me."

The tiny present. I scooped it up from under the tree and put it in front of Sonia.

"Try and guess before you open it," Annie said excitedly.

She considered the object for a few seconds.

"I don't know . . . a bracelet?"

"No . . ."

"A brooch," Pierrot ventured.

"No . . ."

"Is it something you wear?" Sonia asked.

"Kind of. But it doesn't fit everybody."

A bead of sweat blossomed on my forehead and the words *it doesn't fit everybody* echoed in my head. I wanted to leap up and order everyone to stop right there, but the timer was ticking away, the fuse was burning, and there I was, standing and watching, my hands tied.

"Well, I really don't know," Sonia conceded.

"Open it."

"Open it! Open it! Open it!" Pierrot chanted.

Sonia's nervous fingers fiddled with the paper as if she, too, feared some danger. I glanced at Pierrot. Eyes closed, he placed his glass on the table as the wine moved around his mouth. I tried to use telepathy to tell him not to open them, to keep them closed until the end of time. He swallowed the precious liquid and turned in Sonia's direction. When he saw her shattered expression, he lowered his eyes slowly towards the object that lay quietly, not bothering a soul, in its little baby box.

17

When Sonia and Annie got into the Mustang, I realized we'd all gone too far. I was worried, too, because it was pouring rain and Annie, who'd climbed in behind the wheel, seemed to be three sheets to the wind. I went out on the porch and asked them to wait a little, said we should discuss it — among adults anything is possible — but I could only watch as the two doors slammed shut simultaneously and the motor sprung to life. They disappeared into the night, the brakes throwing red lights over the icy road.

Pierrot was lying on his side, on the floor, in front of the fireplace. He was crying like a baby and drinking vinegary Saint-Emilion out of the bottle. I extended my arm towards the outlet and pulled on the cord. I couldn't stand seeing Pierrot that way, completely demolished, in the multi-coloured glow of the Christmas lights. The celestial table sank into darkness. I sat down among the shards of glass and plates.

Actually, I'd had nothing to do with the whole mess. Of course, when Sonia realized what kind of bomb had just exploded in her face, once she'd extracted the pacifier from its little box, she wanted to know who'd given me permission to open my big mouth. She could have turned the whole thing into a joke and tried to conceal the truth; I, for one, would have helped her do just that. But she was too surprised to consider that avenue for even a second. Which is why she went after me in her thoughtless way, as if I were the guy who hadn't known how to pull out in time.

"I thought I could trust you," she told me, shedding her first tear.

That's all it had taken to launch a tremendous chain reaction.

Pierrot crumpled up the wrapping paper from the little box and threw it at the fireplace. The object hit the screen and bounced back in his direction. He lowered his head.

"Why didn't you tell me anything?"

A few moments of silence settled over us. I was walking on hot coals; I'd at least better concentrate.

"Listen, Pierrot," I said in a voice as calm as swamp water. "Sonia came to me asking for advice. I couldn't very well turn her down."

"So you turned me down instead."

"I did what I did because I was looking for a way to tell you without you going haywire, without you getting hurt — don't you see that?"

"You guys didn't succeed."

Obviously we hadn't succeeded. He had raged like a

bull chasing a torero. Not because she was pregnant — because she hadn't thought he was solid enough to tell him. "It's about trust," he repeated ten or fifteen times in the quarter hour that followed the revelation. He paced back and forth across the room as Sonia sat sobbing in her chair. Annie and I spelled each other off, offering her small words of comfort. I know it sounds strange: of the two of them, Pierrot should have needed us most, but he seemed to be doing just fine. Sonia had kept it all inside for so long that when it started coming out, there was no way to stop her. We both tried our best to console her, and every time our eyes met, Annie gave me a poisonous look. A young mother in distress was in the vicinity, so naturally she felt closer to her than to any man.

Pierrot took a big shot of vinegar and made a terrible face. I grabbed the bottle from his hands.

"Don't move, I'll go get us some beers."

Pierrot had paced the room and Sonia had cried her tears, and I knew that we hadn't hit bottom yet. A few minutes later, things took a very bitter turn. Personally, I would have waited, but it was bigger than all of us. Annie asked a simple question, and we lost control over the whole process. We let it take us over completely, as if we were amateurs.

"Think about it," Annie asked, "aren't you just a little pleased to be a father?"

"That's not it," he answered, raising his eyes heavenward. "It's about trust!"

It was more than that, but he didn't know it yet. One look at Sonia, gulping back hard and choking, and I knew it wouldn't be long now.

"He's not the father," she announced, and it was like a ton of bricks falling on a house of cards.

"What?" asked Annie, looking in my direction.

"What do you mean?" Pierrot echoed.

Sonia took her time and told us her story. Mind you, I was in no hurry. I wondered if I'd have time to stow everything that could be thrown at a wall. No such luck; we only had a few more seconds. I decided to hold on to my glass.

"It happened while we were apart, Pierrot. It was an accident, it doesn't mean anything."

Strange — Pierrot showed no reaction. A shadow seemed to cross his face. Meanwhile, Annie looked in all directions at once, her lips moving slightly. She must have been saying *Oh, shit* and *I can't believe this* and other such useless things.

I kept my eyes on Pierrot and tried to gauge his next move, but that was impossible. I had no idea what was going through his head. But I was sure about one thing: he certainly wasn't going to beat Sonia up. That wasn't like him and, besides, Sonia could kill him with her little finger. On the other hand, he could very well get to his feet, put on his coat, and walk to Gabon and start a new life. His reaction, when it did come, had been rather healthy: he took the edge of the tablecloth and began pulling it slowly until everything that had been on the table ended up on the floor in one or several pieces.

I handed him a beer and stood behind him, eyes on the fire. He had stopped crying, but I knew the wound was deep.

"Why couldn't I see she was pregnant?"

"She's no more than four weeks, Pierrot, it's no big thing."

His action had been legitimate. Who could have blamed

him for wanting to wreck something? Unfortunately, he also contributed to the mess. Sonia was looking for something to grasp on to, a way of lifting her head out of the water, and when she saw he was starting to act stupid, she latched onto that.

"Now you know why I didn't want to tell you," she snapped. "You're acting like a four-year-old."

That was a smooth calculation. Now she was back on equal footing with him. Thanks to his desperate action, Pierrot had just assumed half the blame.

"What do you expect?" he shouted, "that I would bow down and kiss the ground you walk on? You wanted to be alone for a few days to clear things up — that was fine. The very next thing you do is treat yourself to the first guy who comes along — that's your choice. But at least you could have been careful!"

I wouldn't have put it quite that way, but I couldn't help agreeing with him.

"I did it to see what I'd feel," she protested. "To see whether I'd think about you, to see whether I really loved you."

"That's funny, I never needed to fuck the first chick who came along to find that out. I asked myself the question, then I answered it."

They were too busy to realize it, but they were professing love to each other in the most beautiful way. When I saw that, I began hoping again.

"But, Pierrot, I felt you inside me the whole time," she sobbed. "I don't even remember him. He wasn't really there, I felt you the whole time."

"So, then," he retorted, "it's like the kid's actually mine."

I said I was beginning to hope. I didn't say it would be easy.

I felt around for my cigarettes; they were on the floor, like everything else. I handed one to Pierrot and stuck one in my mouth. He lit up and gave me the lighter over his shoulder. We both took a deep drag. I looked around as I exhaled, and couldn't help noticing we were in a hell of a mess. We'd really fucked up. Imagine it: among the four of us we had more than a hundred years of maturity, and all we could think of was yelling, "It takes one to know one!"

"What am I going to do?" he sighed.

"I don't know, man. We're going to sit down and figure something out. Don't worry about it."

"I'll never get over it," he said, extracting a piece of dish that had been sticking out of his side for a while.

"Sure, you will, don't talk crap. It'll take some time, but you'll get over it."

"No, Julien. I could never forgive her."

"What's so bad about it?"

"She slept with some asshole!" he bellowed. "Get the picture?"

"Because that was the only way she had to make sure, and she thought about you the whole time — what more do you want?"

"Yeah, that's great, but it's no reason if you ask me. Besides, she's pregnant, too, or have you forgotten?"

"She can always get an abortion."

"She's had two of them already, Julien, and I'm not too sure she'd go in for a third."

Okay, Sonia's not perfect. Why should she be when the rest of us aren't?

"That's easy to say when you're not in her shoes."

"I don't think she'd change her mind about that."

"Well, man, then you've got a choice. Either you leave her, and be a bastard about it, or you accept her, and be a sucker."

We took another sip or two, listened to the fire crackle, and smoked our cigarettes. Slowly, calm returned to our souls. When we looked at things clearly, it was true, he really had no choice. Although it's enough to make you scream and shout and call upon all the saints in heaven to come to your rescue, in the end there's nothing else to do but sit down and analyze the pros and cons — with a cool head.

"You know, Pierrot, babies come from spermatozoa — that's the size of it. Whether it's yours or someone else's, it's the same messy business. You're talking about a viscous little bug with a big tail that swims around blindly every which way. The rest is all in your head. If you want the kid to be yours, it'll be yours."

That was more or less what he had stammered out to Sonia, using different words. But we were too drunk to understand each other, and we went on believing in our own little scenario screening inside our heads. One false move and we would have heard the whistling of knives cutting the air. Then the inevitable happened. Annie decided to take control of things. It wasn't a bad idea because, at the rate we were going, we'd still be there. The only problem was that her scenario was even more twisted than all of ours put together. One minute she looked at me as if to say, "I hope they'll get out of it alive." The next minute she strode up to me with murder in her eyes. I don't know what happened between those two moments; maybe she realized that if I'd mentioned it to her, she would never have bought the pacifier.

She picked some plates off the floor and sent them flying against the wall. We were all so astonished that we didn't lift a finger — we watched the stuff go hurtling past and protected our faces when the explosions got too close to our heads. No doubt there was a message somewhere. When she had reduced everything to dust, including the window pane with the Médoc bottle, she closed her eyes and took a deep breath.

"You're both a couple of assholes, you guys. A couple of perfect assholes."

We tried to figure out what was going on but, so far, we were short of clues. Even Sonia was giving her a strange look.

"You're stupid dumb fucks," she elaborated, "and I wonder what the hell we're doing with you."

Half of me wanted to calm her down, the other half wanted to head for the hills. She was in such a state of rage I was afraid of her.

"You can't understand anything!" she screamed. "We waste our entire lives trying to explain it to you — you never understand a thing!"

I wouldn't have minded a little explanation right then, even if I was starting to think we were all losing our marbles. That's how crimes of passion happen, I thought. The craziest one of the bunch picks up a knife and starts stabbing at the air, hoping to hit something warm-blooded.

"Try to put yourselves in our position," she went on. "We don't control our bodies. One week a month we're practically on our hands and knees, and when our body starts crying for a baby, the message goes straight to our heads and we can't do anything about it."

Unlike Pierrot, who knew nothing of our sexual difficulties, I knew Annie was talking more for herself than for Sonia. Maybe she was right. We don't know anything about the biological clock, all those needs to fulfill, all those hormone waves. They're victims of their bodies. But they keep forgetting that we're their victims. It should even out, if you ask me.

We all stared at each other. There we were, standing, each in his own corner. For a second I thought a microphone was going to descend from the ceiling and a referee appear. No such luck — Annie made the first move. She took Sonia by the hand and led her downstairs.

"Fuck off and die, assholes!"

At first I didn't move. I figured a little time apart would do us good, give us a little food for thought. But when I heard the front door open, I rushed downstairs to try to stop them.

• • •

I picked up the present I'd bought for Pierrot.

"Here," I told him, tearing the wrapping paper. "Merry Christmas."

Painfully, he lifted himself into a standing position. I handed him the package. With a steady hand, he pulled off the metallic paper and the cork, and the top of the bottle formed a little circle under his nostrils. There are few wine lovers who don't appreciate cognac as well.

The girls were out in the night somewhere, driving

who-knows-where, and we were here, with nothing but a load of regrets. We put a few logs on the fire and stretched out on our backs, enjoying the view of the starry sky through the shattered window pane. The rain had stopped falling and the wind gusted cold from time to time. The cognac did what it could, but we still had a bitter taste in our mouths, and I don't think the Saint-Emilion was the only thing to blame.

18

We tried to burn up the road, but unfortunately, even with the pedal to the metal, we could barely break ninety kilometres an hour. Pierrot was nervously chewing on the inside of his lips as his eyes scoured the landscape. We'd been on the road for an hour now, frozen stiff, in the two-degree Celsius air.

The first thing we did when we woke up this morning was void our stomachs. Pierrot kneeled down before the toilet, I turned on the taps to drown out the noise, he sounded the attack, and I followed immediately after him in the sink. I understood why when I discovered the cognac bottle, three-quarters empty.

After a warm shower, we managed to keep down a cup of coffee. We sipped gingerly at it, unsure whether it would stay in our stomachs, but the stuff set us right. I wanted to call the apartment, but the phone had been cut off, so we tried Pierrot's place. There was no answer. We should have known — the girls weren't going to make our lives easy.

Considering our state of health, we cleaned up the house with some efficiency. Pierrot went upstairs with a broom and a few garbage bags while I attacked the kitchen. I was hoping the girls would come back by the time we'd finished cleaning house, but when I picked up the rabbit carcass to dump it in the can, I understood nature's cruelty and knew that hope was in vain. I took it as a warning: from here on in, we'd have to play it tough, since anything could happen.

After the housework, without consultation or a word of conversation, we put on our jackets and went out the door. Just as we were going down the steps, the phone rang. Pierrot stared at me, half-frozen by fear. I realized then that although we were ready to climb on our steeds, unsheathe our swords, and go into battle to get our girlfriends back, we hadn't spent a minute thinking about what we'd say to them. Good thing Annie couldn't see us now, or she'd really call us assholes. The third ring. We sauntered back into the house, hypnotized by the phone, like deer frozen in a car's headlights. I put my hand on the receiver, but couldn't pick it up. Fourth ring. It occurred to me that it might be serious: maybe the police were calling to inform us that the girls had knocked down a row of utility poles. Fifth ring. Like the alarm at a school fire drill, even if we knew it was only a test, the damn noise set our nerves on edge.

"Pick it up, Julien!"

Secretly, I hoped I'd waited long enough, so that when I picked up the receiver, all I'd hear would be someone hanging up on the other end.

"Hello?" I dared.

"You have a call from Nairobi, Kenya," a toneless voice announced. "Do you accept the charges?"

"Of course."

"Julien?" the old man ventured.

"It's me, all right."

"How are things?"

"Fine. And you?"

"Perfecto. I didn't go on the safari. I'll tell you more later. I just called to tell you that everything's okay and that I'll be back on January 2 at four o'clock. Will you be there?"

"You can count on me."

"Is everything okay with you?"

"Just fine."

"Glad to hear it. So I'll see you then. I've got a real surprise for you. I can't wait for you to see it."

"Something African?"

"Originally African."

"Originally?"

"I'll tell you more later. Till then, kiss Annie for me."

"Sure."

"One more thing, Julien."

"What's that?"

"Merry Christmas!"

•••

Just shy of the apartment, I finally let the motor relax. There was no Mustang convertible to be seen. I noticed how repugnant December was with its liquefying dog shit flowing gently across the sidewalks towards the gutters. A perfect reflection of our spirits.

"You think they're still together?" Pierrot asked.

"Annie won't let go of Sonia until this whole business is settled."

"What does she want, anyway? Why was she carrying on like that?"

"You mean Annie?"

"Yeah."

"She wants a kid. She's been on me about it for the last five months. She's run out of ways of convincing me."

Pierrot narrowed his eyes. "You know how this is going to end up? They're going to kill us!"

A small mountain of flyers and bills awaited us from behind the door. It took both of us to push them out of the way. As I walked down the hallway, I thought of the good times Annie and I had had here. Naked, or with our clothes on. We checked out the place: they obviously hadn't been here. Pierrot picked up the phone and dialled his place.

"Phone's dead," I reminded him.

"Oh, yeah, I forgot."

We got back into the old truck and went speeding off downtown. Since it was Christmastime, everyone was walking around with beatific smiles, the drivers were polite the way they never were, they fell over each other trying to let the other guy pass, and there we were, disrupting that harmony by careening through town like madmen, like Santa Claus on bad acid.

Pierrot searched his apartment, looking for a clue that might tell us whether they had been by or not. The stove wasn't warm, nothing had changed in the fridge, the bathtub was dry, and the sinks were, too. But he wouldn't let it go. He paced from one room to the next, chewing on his lips, scratching his scalp.

"I've got it!"

"What?"

"They were here. Sonia was, in any case."

"How's that? What did you find?"

"She picked up some clothes. I knew it, she can't go more than two days wearing the same thing. What do you think," he asked me with a serious look, "where did they go?"

"I have no idea, Pierrot. I don't get it. Annie hardly knows anybody, at least, not anybody she can just show up at and stay with."

"Doesn't she have any family?"

"Her parents have lived in Florida since she was fourteen."

"Sonia doesn't know anybody in town besides Bill and Paule. And she's only met them twice."

"Do you think they could be there?"

"No . . ."

We decided to call anyway. Naturally, there was no answer. They were probably having dinner at Bill's parents' place. Christmas is sacred at their house, the seven kids gather around Mom and Dad, and everybody pretends they're having fun. They have nothing to say to each other, but once a year they have to spend a few hours together anyway.

Our stomachs began to growl. We transferred the contents of the fridge to the kitchen table. A bit of cheese on hard bread, a slice of ham with a fine coating of mayonnaise. We ate half-heartedly, hoping our guts would accept the invasion. After four or five mouthfuls, stuffed like Christmas turkey, we put everything away and Pierrot went back to his pacing.

We had no idea what to do next. We looked up at each

other every once in a while, hoping to see the other guy's eyes light up with revelation. But our faces were like dirty panes of glass, and we went from examining the floor to scrutinizing the window, shrugging our shoulders and sighing like lost souls. After a while we shook off our lethargy enough to go out and buy cigarettes and beer before the stores closed.

Thousands and thousands of tiny lights shone everywhere, every window had a tree, every door a wreath, and the few employees still at their cash registers were busting their jaws trying to smile.

At the corner store, we bought a case of beer and three packs of smokes. An absolutely fabulous girl served us, twenty-six or twenty-seven years old, dark hair, black eyes, a Latin smile. Unfortunately, we were in no mood to appreciate her. We handed her the money and she gave us back the change with champagne sparkles in her eyes, thank you very much and Merry Christmas to both of you. Merry Christmas, my ass, I thought to myself as the door chimes rang out behind us.

"Did you see the smile that chick had on?" Pierrot declared. "I bet that in a few minutes she's going to close up shop and meet her boyfriend and spend the most beautiful Christmas of her life with him."

"What are you trying to do, man, kill me?"

19

We hunkered down at Pierrot's place and spent the week making phone calls and unannounced visits to places where we thought they might be. We turned ourselves inside out trying to find a theory that would stand up, but we came up with nothing. I called all the hospitals in town; no one reported any news of them. When Pierrot suggested we visit all the hotels and motels, I accused him of insanity and tapped my right temple that was half-covered with greasy hair.

Besides that, we did fuck-all. Once or twice a day, we nibbled on some cold food. The only thing we bothered heating up was a pair of knives to smoke a few crumbs of hash, hoping it would help us get some sleep. We both looked like mental cases who had just stepped out of electroshock therapy. We couldn't take five steps without getting a cramp in our legs or a stabbing pain in our hearts.

Our guts turned flip-flops and stress never gave us a moment's rest. Pain was our shadow; looking in the mirror was a horrifying experience. We were in such bad shape someone should have organized a telethon to help us out. But they would have wasted their time, and in any case, even with all the money in the world, we wouldn't live to see the end of the year.

At some point I thought of Dalida, but I didn't have the strength to go all the way out there. I pictured the poor cow with her udders as swollen as a hot-air balloon, keeping watch over the barn door and praying to the version of the Baby Jesus that looks after cows. I couldn't leave her like that, so I summoned up what courage I had and, thanks to Information, called the general store in the village. I invented a completely senseless story. Pierrot was doubled up laughing in his chair while I laid on the bullshit, as serious as can be. The old ladies agreed to help out, but it was just to keep from hearing my pitiful string of lies. That didn't matter. They'd look in on Dalida once a day until further notice.

Besides our impromptu visits, we didn't leave the house. We even had the beer delivered, along with unfiltered Gitanes. We had never smoked French cigarettes in our lives, but we were ready to do anything to suffer. The idea was to ingest as many toxic substances as possible. We even stooped so low as to watch *Dallas*. That's how desperate we were.

We kept the curtains closed the whole time, so we never really knew whether it was day or night, if it was Tuesday, Wednesday, or the weekend. Sometimes we would turn on the television and, according to what was on, decide what time it should be. Only problem was that, half the time, we got the test patterns. They didn't help us much, though the plot was easy to follow. We sat down in front of it with empty eyes, and the TV would engulf us in colour and a kind of sound, and we would mix it all up in our brains and make images out of it. It was true interactive television, but don't tell the authorities about it; they'll find some way to screw it up.

I dreamed of Annie every time I managed to close my eyes — that was the hardest part. Annie naked, Annie climbing on top of me, Annie shooting at me. Naturally, when I hit bottom, I started thinking of Florence again. In a strange way, those pictures made me want to fight on and keep on struggling. She was the only one who could breathe a little life into me. I took that as a positive sign. We weren't out of the woods yet, but I could see that we might come through.

Besides the old ladies from the general store, the only communication we had with the outside world happened yesterday — or was it the day before? The telephone rang and, to be honest, we were in such bad shape it never occurred to us that it might be Annie or Sonia. We had sunk so deep in our shithole we'd forgotten how we'd gotten there in the first place.

"Hello," Pierrot whimpered.

"I'd like to speak to Pierre, please."

"Speaking."

"Oh, yes, well, I've been looking through Sonia's portfolio and I'd be interested in meeting you or her."

Suddenly, Pierrot started acting human. He sat up straight on his chair and ran his hand through his hair.

"That could be arranged, only Sonia doesn't meet with just anyone."

That's when I understood he must have invented all kinds of stories to round out her resumé.

"We're not just anyone, I assure you. We'd be willing to give her a small part of our next ready-to-wear collection. I should tell you that the opportunity opened up because one of our designers bowed out, but it's still a very good chance for Sonia. The presentation is scheduled for the autumn season, the end of August."

"Ladies' clothing?"

"Yes. Our maternity line."

Pierrot's smug look literally fell to pieces and crashed to the floor. He looked at me; his right eyebrow rose.

"Well, all right, I'll talk to her about it and call you back."

He noted down a name and number on a scrap of paper, said good-bye, and gently returned the receiver to the cradle.

"Go heat up the knives," he told me.

•••

Our hearts weren't in it, but it was too late, we'd given our word — Bill and Paule were counting on us. We ordered a case of beer, more Gitanes, and a bag full of disposable razors. It took us each a good hour to scrub ourselves clean and rid ourselves of the fungus that had crept over our faces. Naturally, Pierrot got into the shower first, which meant I was stuck with lukewarm water. Once we got going and picked up a little momentum, our blood climbed back into our brains again and things started returning to normal. Despite the fatigue and worry and madness that hovered over us like a cloud, we began living again.

I opened a few windows and even the frigid air of the year's first day couldn't keep us from strutting around naked. We wanted to rejoin the world again. Pretty soon we had cleaned up the apartment and even washed some of our clothes. We were ready for anything, open to any experience. We even turned on the radio. The squawk box tortured our ears with Christmas music for almost two hours, but we stood our ground and didn't give in. A second skin had grown over us during the week, a skin as solid and impermeable as rubber, and nothing could touch us. Or at least that's what we wanted to think.

We climbed into the truck, stopped off to pick up two bottles of wine, being careful to avoid any vinegary Saint-Emilions, then headed towards Bill and Paule's seven-and-a-half-room apartment.

•••

We shuffled our shoes on the mat to keep the snow out of the hall, then eased our way towards the din that came from the end of the corridor. When we were level with the bathroom, the door swung open hard and the doorknob crashed against my right hip.

"Oops," Bill grunted as his yellow head filled the door frame.

He smiled. I grimaced in pain. We shook hands and exchanged New Year's greetings.

"Follow me," he called, relieving us of the bottles. "Everyone's in the kitchen. I tried to get them into the living room, but they won't listen to me."

The kitchen was the keystone of the apartment. The room was something like ten metres by eight. They knocked down a wall to get it that way. The table could seat ten people easily, fourteen if you squeezed in. Besides that, there were long counters that you could set your butt down on and admire the view of the river through the majestic windows.

I didn't recognize anybody except Paule, the mother-to-be to whom the party was dedicated. She was leaning against the window, as radiant as a pulsar. She called my name and opened her arms. I never could resist her creamy skin; I ran to her to take a bite of it.

"I got what I wanted," she whispered into my ear.

"Don't come complaining if it doesn't work out."

"I owe it to you in a way. I want you to know that."

"Please, spare me."

Pierrot also showed up to sample the light vanilla perfume hidden behind her earlobes.

"Congratulations."

"What about me?" Bill asked indignantly. "Why isn't anyone congratulating me? I did half the work."

"You don't deserve congratulations, man — you deserve condolences."

I yelled that one so loud that everyone burst out laughing. Then I put my reasonable voice back on so as not to get people's hopes up too high. Conversations resumed, although there were a few smiles on those in the know.

Bill opened the fridge door. "What are you drinking?"

"We're into beer," Pierrot explained.

"Local, imported, dark, light, red?"

"The strongest you got," I said, pulling my pack of Gitanes from my pocket.

"Come and put your coats in the bedroom," Paule said, taking us both by the hand.

We held fast to her and she led us to the very spot where, most likely, the little beast she carried inside her had been conceived. The same view of the river. We threw our coats on the pile.

"Paule," Pierrot whispered, "can I ask you something?"

"Anything."

When Paule said *anything* to Pierrot, it wasn't just a figure of speech.

"I want to see your stomach."

"Of course," she answered, lifting her dress to just below her breasts, displaying her panties and a perfectly flat belly.

"That's it?"

"Of course. I'm only three weeks pregnant. What did you expect?"

I thought the same way Paule did, except I would have added "dumb-ass" at the end of my sentence. I knew what Pierrot was after. He wanted the assurance that it was normal for him not to have noticed Sonia's stomach. If Paule was as flat as a board at three weeks, Sonia couldn't have been much bigger at four.

We filed out of the room just as Bill arrived, beers in hand. He herded us back into the kitchen to introduce us to everyone. He does that every time. He hasn't figured out yet that we find it difficult making friends with normal people. And vice versa. He tried his luck again this time, as if our status as freaks tortured him. We held onto our bottles good and tight and began at the beginning. What's-His-Name, meet Thingamajig. Thingamajig, this is What's-His-Name. Thingamajig is Mr. Nobody's best friend. Mr. Nobody is Hey You's husband, who's also Say What's lover. Hello, buenos dïas, bonjour.

"Let me show you something, Julien," Bill told me after we'd gone once around the room.

"What's that?"

"You'll see."

I followed him down the hall. Bill's crazy about computers. The machines pay the rent on the apartment and they bought him a brand new car. He's a genius of a kind. We walked into his work space, which was the first room to the left after the front door.

"The office bought me a new toy."

I made the mistake the first time I set foot in his room: I asked him a few questions about the hardware. What followed was a two-hour demonstration of all the electronic wonders, how if you pushed this button that thing would happen. Since then, every time I come here, he puts me through the same business because I'm the only one who hasn't told him to shut up yet.

"Look," he said, his voice quivering, "isn't it wonderful?"

"It's not bad. But mine is bigger and it's made out of wood."

"Don't be stupid. It's not a TV set, it's a monitor."

"What does it have that the three others don't?"

"I can give it a command just by putting my finger on the screen. Look."

He turned on the computer, pushed a few buttons, waited a few seconds, then pushed a few more.

"I hate to contradict you, Bill, but you're touching the keyboard, not the screen."

"I know," he sighed. "Wait a minute, would you?"

Four little pictures appeared on the screen. A dog, a cat, a horse, and a mouse.

"Congratulations! Did you draw them all by yourself?"

"Yeah, but it's just an experiment. I'm making a program for my son. Go ahead, touch one of the pictures."

I like dogs, so that's the one I touched.

"I am a dog," a synthetic voice announced.

"What do you think?"

"It's sad, Bill."

"What's sad?"

"My beer is empty."

"Try the other ones. I'll get you a refill."

"I am a horse," the voice let on when I touched the horse.

I hate cats, but I touched it anyway.

"I am a cat."

Then I touched the screen everywhere except on the picture.

"Error. Please try again," the voice suggested.

I stopped. It was completely ridiculous. I swivelled the chair in the direction of the river and thought of the poor kid born to serve as a guinea pig for a whole battery of tests, all more mind-numbing than the rest. One day, someone would shake his hand, and the poor thing would say, "I am a hand."

What the hell was Bill doing with my beer? I decided to investigate, but someone was coming through the front door. I had no choice; I had to wait. Feet were stamped, soles scraped, boots removed. Then the door closed again, opening my field of vision.

The first thing I wanted to do was throw my arms around them and cover them with kisses. But if I stopped a moment to ponder the hellish week I'd just spent, I still would have thrown my arms around them — around their necks.

Pierrot chose that moment to come strolling out of the kitchen. He found himself face to face with them, seven or eight metres away. We had no idea of what they'd been through the last week. What made us so sure they hadn't returned to blow us away?

Annie took my hand discreetly and came to my side in the office doorway. Sonia was standing nearby, while Pierrot was still at the far end of the hallway, legs slightly spread, arms hanging along his sides. One of them would have to draw first. A loud, violent report rang out. I closed my eyes. It was Bill throwing open the bathroom door.

"Hi, girls," he bellowed. "You're early."

That's why nobody asked us any questions. They were all in it together. Bill came up and kissed Sonia, then Annie. I took advantage of the diversion to free my beer from his hand.

"I'll leave you now," he said and headed back to the kitchen.

As he went past, he closed the bathroom door, revealing Pierrot again, standing motionless. Slowly, Sonia moved towards him, her eyes fastened onto his, then she took his hand timidly and led him into the bedroom. Annie guided me into the office and closed the door behind us.

"Listen," she began, "I don't want to get into a shouting match."

"Neither do I."

"But I have some things I want to tell you, and I want you to listen to me all the way through."

"Go ahead," I said, taking her head in my hands.

"First of all, I'm sorry, I don't know what came over me, I completely lost my head, I didn't know what I was saying."

"Uh-huh," I moaned, crushing her lips with mine.

Two seconds later, I had her entire mouth. She offered her body to mine, and I felt her sex against my thigh.

"I want to stay with you," she whispered into my ear. "Till the end of my life."

I pressed a little harder against her, and we stumbled over to Bill's worktable. There's nothing like two pairs of jeans rubbing together. It's stiff, and there's a protuberance just below the rivet that's worth lingering over.

"There's only one thing," she went on, as best she could, "if we really want to be good together, if we really want to live in peace . . ."

She kept her breath, she didn't lose her head. I'll never know how she managed. I'd been floating ever since we got in this room.

"Do you hear me? We absolutely, positively . . ."

I slipped my hand between us to undo her pants. Her panties gave me a wink. I pushed everything down below her knees.

"And this is no joke," she sighed.

I put my hands under her backside and lifted her high enough to sit on the table. The look on her face changed. Her mouth hung open. She threw her head backwards, half-closed her eyes, and slipped her hands inside my pants.

"It's essential," she whispered, "if we want to stay together for a long, long time . . ."

She made quick work of my jeans, leaving my cock to flap like a flag in a stiff breeze. I pushed one of her breasts through the top of her T-shirt.

"Like I said," she went on, "it's absolutely fundamental . . ."

Then she thrust me into her, all the way to the hilt. In a single movement. A single, majestic movement, I'd call it. We were so excited that the slightest movement brought cries of pleasure from our lips. Our mouths devoured each other, thoughtlessly, completely mad. I moved from one breast to the other like a bulimic who's got a veal shoulder in one hand and a leg of lamb in the other.

"Absolutely, absolutely, you understand . . . we have to have a kid together, otherwise I'm leaving."

Her words sounded like all the other obscenities you whisper into each other's ears when you're tearing up the bedsprings. They were no more important than the squeaking of the table legs that worked to our rhythm. Music, all of it. Our bodies were composing a fugue, a suite, a symphonic poem. And now it was happening, exploding everywhere, the fireworks all blowing at once, a second big bang shooting forth millions of sparks. Blown away by the explosion, drained of all energy, our bodies exhausted as our minds galloped on in darkness, we crashed out on top of Bill's stuff.

"Error. Please try again," the synthetic voice suggested.

PART 4

20

"Do you need help?"

"No. Thanks anyway, but I've done this hundreds of times."

Actually, I was asking just to be polite — I knew very well that Azalée never needs anything. I was more worried about the old man. I'd already tasted his cooking, and I know what that can be like. Fortunately, he was following her directions to the letter, without a dash of personal initiative. Not a drop went into the mixture without Azalée first checking it down to the most minute measure. That made me feel a lot more secure. I don't mind trying out new culinary experiences, as long as we stay on the right side of good taste. And I like the idea that, from time to time, someone is willing to knock themselves out for a whole day just to serve a few dishes that can stand up to the taste test. That was Azalée's contribution.

All six of us were crashed out in the living room, watching them work. Sonia, Paule, and Annie were stretched out on the floor, while Bill, Pierrot, and I shared the couch. We listened to the click-clack of knives slicing through vegetables, the tlick-tlick of ladles moving through pots, and the huh-huh of girls rehearsing their deliveries.

An African-style meal was a great idea. It was for a good cause — to celebrate the work we'd completed over the last five days. Honestly, I never thought it would be possible. I told myself, *watch out, he's gone off his rocker, it's no good for him to have a young thing in his bed, he's starting to think he possesses life eternal*. Okay, I'm exaggerating a little. An addition is not the end of the world, but I couldn't understand why he wanted another room when he had a perfectly good one upstairs.

"That's all there is to it!" he had hollered. "I'm not going up there anymore. Can you get that through your head?"

Sure, I understood it, but I thought he was laying it on too thick. When Florence died, I swore off a lot of things, but I didn't burn my bed just because she'd slept in it!

"I lived forty years with that woman," he went on. "Forty years, boy! You try and love someone more than half your life. And I didn't just fuck her when I had the time — I loved her!"

That hurt. It was obvious he was talking about Flo and me. You love the best way you know how to, damnit! Go screw yourself, Granddad.

"Anyway, I haven't told you the half of it, so how could you understand?"

"All right, already," I laughed. "We'll build you your extra room, so stop whimpering."

We spent more than a month figuring it all out, designing the room, and shopping for the best prices. Once we finally got our hands on everything we needed, I decided it would be a good idea to hear what Bill had to say. In thirty minutes, he revamped everything it took us thirty days to devise. The only difference was that his design wouldn't fall down.

We got down to work on Wednesday, and today everything was complete. The skies were favourable and the April sun kept us warm without sapping our strength.

Our beautiful extension sat adjacent to the living room. We could be proud of it; we'd worked like pros. The old man, even if he wasn't much good with blueprints, could hammer in a nail. Pierrot did everything he was told, and did it on the double, and I passed the boards, picked up the tools, gathered up the screws. We decided that would be my job after I dropped a hammer from up in the rafters, grazing Bill's right ear. The girls hung around, helping us with their comments, giving words of encouragement, and telling us to be careful. At mealtime, they made sandwiches and served them with lemonade and, later, beer. All in all, it had been a real masculine experience.

•••

"Who wants something to drink?"

Annie leaned forward on her elbows and turned her two big sunny eyes in my direction.

"I'll have another Perrier. What about you, Sonia, another Perrier?"

Of course. Ever since Annie started working on her own personal embryo, they fussed over each other night and day. Pierrot and I talked it over and came to the conclusion that they were doing it as a kind of training, a practice, a warm-up, so they'd be perfectly maternal when the little creatures arrived.

"Yes, please. But not too much ice and no lemon. It turns to vinegar in my stomach."

"Did you understand that, Julien?" Annie asked me.

"I think so."

Since they were sure we couldn't fathom anything of what they were going through, they assumed we couldn't understand anything else.

I turned to Pierrot. "What about a Perrier?"

"Sure. But hold the ice, the lemon, and the Perrier. A beer'll do."

Bill volunteered to give me a hand. On my way to the fridge, I glanced into the pots, just to make sure there weren't any billy goat's eyes or beards floating around.

"What are we eating, anyway?"

Azalée flashed me her incredible smile, a chasm of a mouth that opened onto two strong rows of incontestably white, symmetrical teeth.

"I'm not telling you. You'll find out soon enough."

That's the way she is: nothing's simple with her, everything has to be a surprise. She's been that way ever since she arrived. Actually, she already lived here; she just hadn't come into our lives yet. She knocked us flat on our asses, I must say. We showed up at the airport to pick up the old man after New Year's. When the flight from Nairobi touched down, we were upstairs, with two or three other whites and a big gang of Africans with smiles as wide as slices of canteloupe. As soon as the first travellers appeared, shouting broke out from all quarters, drum beats were heard, and one couple even executed a few dance steps. Finally, I said to myself, a little heat in this damned winter.

That's when Granddad appeared, preceded by a young African woman wrapped in a multicoloured dress. They exchanged a few words now and again as they waited to go through customs. I figured they were indulging in the usual travellers' chat: "Did you have the chicken or the beef for dinner?" "I had the beef, of course, don't you remember? I was right behind you in the line outside the toilet to throw up."

Then we beheld a miracle. We stood and stared, it was unbelievable — we had to pinch each other to make sure we weren't dreaming. It was statistically impossible, but it happened all the same: Granddad's luggage was the first to come rolling out on the conveyor belt.

He finally came out once the formalities were done. I waved my arms so he'd see us in this sea of black.

"Hello!" he called, and it sounded like a sigh of relief.

I thought his features looked drawn, and wondered if he'd brought us back some exotic microorganism. We hugged each other, he kissed Annie, I introduced Pierrot and Sonia, he was glad to meet them. Meanwhile, a young African woman stood behind him with an ivory smile and caviar eyes.

"I promised you a typically African souvenir . . ."

She took two steps forward.

"This is Azalée."

And they both dissolved into peals of obscene laughter as the rest of us stood there with our mouths open.

The bags were stowed in the Mustang, we squeezed

onto the seats, and Sonia drove us home under a metallic January sky. The old man asked us the usual stupid questions about what had happened while he'd been gone. Nothing much, Granddad. The plot unfolding on the back seat interested us more. What was that graceful black hand doing in that old, white, wrinkled palm?

"Did you meet in Africa?" I finally asked.

"No," the old man answered. "On the way over, we had seats together."

Azalée looked at us with a hint of apprehension in her eyes. Then she decided to speak.

"That's right. He told me he was going on a safari."

"What did you think about that?" I asked, stoking the fire.

"'You old fool,' I told him."

She opened her mouth wide and volcanic laughter poured from the centre of her being. We couldn't help laughing ourselves.

"When it was all over," she concluded with a laugh, "he didn't use his gun a single time. Not the one for hunting, that is . . ."

She let loose with another explosion, a completely vulgar one this time, and turned her big black eyes in his direction.

She insisted on showing him the country, instead of letting him shoot off his rifle at a bunch of poor, defenceless animals. She knew what she was doing. She laid the trap of his life for him and he walked right into it like a neophyte. She served up the oldest clichés in the book and he didn't suspect a thing. She even had them run out of gas in the bush. Result: they spent the last five days in bed. You can imagine, he never stood a chance.

•••

"Okay, time to eat."

Naturally, Annie and Sonia sat down side by side. Regular Siamese twins. They probably even piss together.

"What you see before you is an Algerian salad. There's cucumber, peppers, green olives, coriander, and mint."

"You from Algeria?" Pierrot wanted to know.

"No, Zaire. But Algeria is in Africa."

"If you say so."

We all tucked into the salad, even the old man, who doesn't particularly like vegetables. I wasn't surprised, since Azalée has him on a leash. It's incredible, becoming enslaved to a woman one-third his age. He practically eats out of her hand. She could convince him the moon was blue. She makes him clean the house once a week, and when I say clean, I mean everything, the walls, the windows, everything! She's obsessed with cleanliness. And fucking, too. I can't imagine the pleasure she gets from sleeping with a wrinkled-up old guy. I can understand why someone might want to live with Granddad, but going to bed with him — that's beyond the capacity of my imagination. If I've told him once, I've told him a thousand times: "A girl who can't stop fucking a guy forty years her senior, and in the most salacious positions, and then who tells him after it's all over to wash down the joint with Chlorox — now that's just not natural. She's got to be hiding something." But the old man doesn't say a thing, he just rolls up his sleeves and scrubs the place down every week. Otherwise, she won't sleep over. There is one advantage to that: he knows just what to do whenever he wants a little time to himself. Still, he's not exactly getting shortchanged, since Azalée is a hell of a woman. She shines, from the inside out.

I looked around the table to make sure everyone had what they needed. They were all grazing away happily. When the eight of us are together, silence is a rare commodity. Someone always feels the need to pipe up with some kind of nonsense. Though, actually, we've been a quiet bunch lately, very well behaved. We've developed our own little habits, as individuals and as a group. As if we needed to set down a solid base, and dig in, probably because the next few months would bring changes that could seriously shake our foundations.

"Hey, everybody," Sonia shouted. "I have an announcement."

"What now?" Pierrot asked immediately, frowning.

"I'm going to be a model in the fashion show."

"Great!" Annie applauded.

"One of the girls changed her mind, so I stepped in. We want to have women who are really pregnant."

Pierrot took a deep breath and held her gaze. "You'll be just about due. I don't know if it's the right thing to do. Did you ask your doctor about it?"

"No one knows better than I do whether I have the strength or not. I'm getting tired of you always coming back to that."

Obviously, there's no sense asking a pregnant woman to understand other people; they have to understand her. We all knew why Pierrot asked the question. It had nothing to do with strength; he was worried about her. She had categorically refused to have an ultrasound. Hearing that little heart beating at top speed was evidence enough. We tried to make her listen to reason, but she wouldn't budge. It's not necessary, she told us, women have been getting along without it for thousands of years. There's no reason for me to have one, who says it can't do any harm to the baby? Annie sat at the other extreme: she kept asking for more photos of our daughter. But she did encourage us to understand Sonia's point of view. They stuck together, whatever the issue.

Besides which, they did spend most of their time together. Now that Sonia was working on her collection, she couldn't stand having Pierrot looking over her shoulder and shouting *Bravo!* every time she drew a line, so she asked him to give her a little space. Annie offered more discreet companionship. They got to share the exaltation of those precious moments together. We gave them all the space they wanted. We came around when it was time to pat their tummies, and massage them, and blurt out the worst clichés with our mouths pressed against their bellies, and endure their crises and moments of intense doubt, but when it came time for a little fun, they preferred to be alone.

So Pierrot helped me and Granddad in the market, we hung out together in the evening, and when they called, we had the right to go see them. They were the kind of girls who give themselves one hundred percent, they didn't hold back from commitment — we had understood that a long time ago. Sonia spent most of her time in her studio, checking everything twice, trying things on, making adjustments. Annie followed one step behind. She held her pin cushion and sharpened her pencils, but her real job was to keep Sonia's spirits up. They were full of plans about what they'd do after the birth, they bought baby clothes and other new-mother things.

Still, I did notice a few differences between them. Annie was completely into the present, into being pregnant. She was always in front of the mirror, admiring her little belly that was just beginning to show and her breasts that grew a little heavier each day. How proud she looked! A day didn't go by without her coming naked to me and asking what I thought. I had to tell her — I couldn't very well lie — that the very thought of her got me hard. I knew I was encouraging her, but what could I do? She was so happy, there was so much light in her eyes that she bowled over every guy she saw.

It was different for Sonia. When she examined herself in the mirror, it was like she was trying to comprehend what was happening to her. At first she wouldn't admit that she couldn't get into the same old pair of jeans. Pierrot did what he could to get her into the mood, but he had his limits, too. And everyone knew why.

"I'd like to make a toast," the old man declared, pushing his chair back, "a toast to the woman who made this marvellous meal."

All right!

"I'd like to make a toast, too," Azalée returned the favour, "a toast to the guys who built us this beautiful new bedroom."

All right!

"I'm going to make a toast, too," I chimed in, "to the girls who are busy cooking us up a new batch of rug rats."

All right!

Then a second miracle occurred. The first one had taken place two weeks earlier and even if it was more of the same, it seemed to us like another blessing. Paule stuck her fork into her salad, and as she was steering the morsel towards her mouth, a look of fear blew across her face. Next thing we knew she was wearing a beatific smile as her fork glanced off the edge of the table and fell under her chair. We all gaped at her, trying to figure out what was going on. She looked at Sonia, who had become a kind of mother for her and Annie. After all, she was experiencing everything before them.

"Did he move?"

"Yes," she cooed.

We all lined up to touch it, one after the other, like a bunch of assholes. Obviously, we didn't feel a thing. Even the mother could hardly sense the first kicks, but we wanted it so bad that a gas pain would have done the trick. Bill got out his notebook and wrote down the date and time, as he had for all the other steps. Annie's eyes immediately filled with tears. She was eager to enter into the privileged circle, and knew it wouldn't be long. Azalée gazed at the old man. Her head dropped seductively to one side. She was as keyed up as a chocomaniac on Easter morning.

"No way," he grumbled.

21

We were all sitting there with stunned smiles on our faces. Meanwhile, inside, fear twisted our guts. They'd been promenading down the runway for the last half hour. At first I kept my eyes peeled. I watched them strut their stuff, and tried to figure out the variations, and decide for myself what I liked — then everything degenerated and all I could do was imagine them naked.

Every time the announcer described a new set of clothes, a murmur of voices rose in the room. All right, I admit it, some pieces were nicely done. The colour, the cut, the length, all the details worked well together. As for the rest, I wouldn't even make my worst enemy — the French poodle — wear those outfits.

Sonia's career was on the line. It was soar or sink. The director of the organization had told us that everything was perfect, and that our protégée had done more than honourable work considering her experience. That had been backstage, just before the show, where we'd gathered to lend our support to Sonia, who was nauseated beyond belief. By then, the woman had realized that everything Pierrot had told her about Sonia was pure invention. But she'd decided to give her a chance anyway, for which we were all deeply grateful.

"Ladies and gentlemen, it's my pleasure to introduce you to a dozen young women who took *their* pleasure a little too freely over the past few months. And now they have to wear the kind of clothes inspired by gamblers who walk out of a saloon wearing a barrel."

Well, that's more or less what she said.

The first three ensembles featured a design that adapted to the stomach as it grew. Nothing exceptional about that, except for once the style was not a complete travesty. The reaction was wonderful. We stood on our chairs, we wanted more, more.

Then Sonia strutted in, both hands on the small of her back, her pelvis out, and her belly about to explode. What a smile! The lighting man could have cut all the spotlights and we would have seen her clear as day. She looked as though she were about to give birth to the sun, and a little light was slipping through the pores of her skin. Naturally, when they introduced her as the designer, applause broke out from everywhere — half of it provided by Pierrot. Annie's expression was priceless, tears of admiration filling her eyes. She kept squeezing my hand, wiping her eyes, then squeezing my hand again with her wet fingers.

Sonia strolled twice across the stage, then stepped onto the wide runway that led into the audience. That's when her million-dollar smile turned into a terrible twist of pain. Nervously, her hands jumped to her stomach and she let out a little cry of distress. A gasp ran through the room. Sonia looked down; her white overalls were stained from her thigh to her feet with a brownish-green liquid. We froze in a deadly silence, which was broken by Pierrot as he leaped from his chair. That set everything into motion. Everyone started breathing again, running in every direction like high-speed circus roustabouts tearing down the big top.

Sonia was on her knees on the stage. Her eyes were glazed.

"I'm afraid, Pierrot, I'm afraid . . ."

He took her hand. "It'll be all right, I'm telling you, we'll take care of everything, don't worry. Does it hurt? No? Good, it's nothing serious, of course it's abnormal, why would you do it any other way? You're not like other people."

"Are you a doctor?" the announcer asked.

"No," he answered, raising his eyes to her. "I'm the father."

"Don't worry, dear," she turned to smile reassuringly at Sonia. "You're not alone. We'll look after everything."

Of course she wasn't alone. The models' partners were all trained for it; they were waiting for their day to dawn, too. So you can imagine, if we all got together, we could move Sonia out of there in a hurry.

Strangely, the other pregnant women kept their distance and looked away with discreet displeasure. I said nothing, but saw the whole thing as a major lesson. If women thought more about times like these, maybe they'd hassle us less with their obsessions. But even that wouldn't change their minds, since most of them want to start all over again at the first possible opportunity. Unbelievable —

us guys stand around with our dicks swinging between our legs and we can't bring ourselves to say no. Even if they vomit every morning for the first three months, even if they won't be able to move for the last two, even if they spend their afternoons at some specialist's getting their insides felt up, even if they tear their crotches in two giving birth and scream like witches on the pyre, they'll come back for more. What do we do? Pull out our little dicks and get to work. Because we like it, because without them we're nothing, we're assholes, we're not worth a dime.

"Stand back," Pierrot ordered. "Let her breathe. Don't worry, it'll work out, we'll get you to the hospital."

"Yeah," I said, "I'll go get the car. I'll be back in a minute."

"If you don't mind," a woman offered timidly, "my husband can drive you. He's a policeman."

Excellent idea. It would take me an hour just to get the key into the ignition. I told Annie to go with them while I took care of the car. She and Pierrot moved slowly through the room, propping up Sonia. Just before Pierrot went out the door, he turned around. But the crowd was too dense for him to spot me in it. Don't worry about me, man, I'll be with you in a flash, don't worry at all, everything'll go down just fine, hundreds go through this every day. Remember, one thing about Sonia, she's got a bulldozer for a brain, which means she can fight her way out of any kind of ditch. She won't fail you, just follow her and hold her tight like a little white stone, like a good-luck charm.

Finally I made my way outside. The air was unusually warm, even for the last day of August. The Mustang was only a couple minutes away, and I decided to run the last ten metres. I jumped into the beast and fired her up. She started like a dream, softly purring, a prayer begging you to give her a little gas and let her play in the traffic.

A few seconds later I was heading for the hospital. I felt at one with the metal and its fusionary process, and my mind was already in the waiting room, pacing the halls and lighting one cigarette off the other.

She was taken by surprise, that's all. Nothing strange about that. As far as I knew, everything was going according to plan. I had no reason to worry. I remembered something about the greenish colour, but I didn't know what; they'd mentioned it in the prenatal classes and it didn't seem to be the end of the world.

The light switched to yellow, but luck was on my side. I put the pedal to the metal and the response was instantaneous. The needle pulled away from eighty and headed for a hundred. Twenty seconds later, a cop car was on my tail with the standard issue flashing lights and wailing siren. I pulled over, glimpsing the hospital through the windshield.

The guy got out of the cruiser. As I watched him in the rearview mirror, I realized I'd seen him before. The last time, he was carrying a chest of drawers on his shoulder. I rolled down my window, damning everything I could.

He removed his hat, leaned his forearm on the frame, and stuck his head in through the window.

"Hi," I said. "I'm sorry, I know, I was going a little fast, but my best friend's girlfriend is at the hospital, she's going to give birth."

He burst out laughing. I didn't know what to think. A laughing cop is like a smoking volcano; it can blow up in your face at any time.

"Driver's licence, registration, insurance, please."

"Right away," I answered, realizing that my licence was back in the truck.

I took the other papers out of the glove compartment and handed them to him, trying to figure out how to tell him about the licence.

"This isn't your vehicle?"

"No, it belongs to the girl who's giving birth right now. She went with a policeman, I took her car, there were four of us, she's a fashion designer, she was presenting her first collection tonight, and we were so excited that . . ."

"Okay, that'll do," he interrupted me. "What about your driver's licence?"

"It's in my truck — I always leave it there, never drive anything else. I completely forgot about it."

"I suppose you have an explanation for the alcohol on your breath, too?"

"Yes and no. I had a couple of beers during the fashion show, you know, all those fabulous girls strutting their stuff make you thirsty."

It was all incredibly vulgar, but I absolutely had to lower myself to the guy's level. Besides, it was working. He smiled.

"I know what it's like. My wife poses naked for the magazines."

Yeah, sure. And I give surfing lessons at a nudist camp for golden agers.

"Wow," I said, "you must have your hands full!"

"You bet. Sometimes, believe it or not, I can't wait to get to work. It's the only way I can get a little rest."

"A lot of guys must envy you."

"I know." Then he gave me a closer look and frowned. "Say, don't we know each other from somewhere?"

"I don't think so."

"Didn't you come to my house once, about a year ago, looking for a girl . . . Annie was her name."

"Oh, yeah, it's all coming back to me. Didn't you throw a chest of drawers at me?"

"Yeah, that's it!"

"I understand why now. A week after she moved in with me, I got home one night, no more Annie, and no more stereo, either. They'd both disappeared, gone up in smoke. I didn't even press charges. I knew no one would ever see her again."

"I'm not surprised," he said, his eyes misting over. "I should have warned you instead of throwing furniture. Excuse me, I have to check something."

Slowly, he walked away, shaking his head. Fifteen long minutes later, he returned.

"I'm sorry, but I've got no choice. You have to come with me to the station."

"What?"

"You have to come with me. Just a formality, nothing important, it'll just take a few minutes."

"Why, what's the matter? I don't have my licence, that's all! Give me a ticket and we'll forget about it. It's that simple, isn't it? What's the big deal? You're here to hand out tickets and I'm here to pay them. Since when does a person have to go down to the station for every single thing? My best friend's having a baby and all you can think of is taking me to the station!"

"Are you finished?"

"Yes, as a matter of fact, I am."

"Sorry, I don't have a choice. You're not in the computer."

That was one excuse I couldn't take. It's like a sickness: you go to the bank, the teller's seen you every week for the last ten years, but as soon as the computer's memory shuts down, hers does, too. It's the same everywhere. Those damned machines are running us, and no one can do anything about it when they blow a fuse.

"Park over there. I'll wait for you in the car."

•••

I'd been locked up in a little office with two chairs and a desk for the last hour and a quarter. "I'll go get us some coffees. I'll be right back." Right back, my ass. As I waited, I couldn't help thinking of all the stories that go around, how they kick the hell out of you, just for fun, in between bites on a doughnut. When life jumps the tracks, the way it was doing now, anything can happen, so you might as well expect the worst. Two hours ago, I was minding my own business, drinking a beer, and watching the girls go by. Now I'm dying of thirst and hoping everybody here got up on the right side of the bed this morning.

Then he showed up with two cups of coffee. "Sorry, I had a phone call."

I bet he was sorry. Like, we're real good friends now, now that we've ridden in a car together. I was sitting in the back like a dog in the dog-catcher's van while he went on and on about Annie, and at every red light the passers-by stared in my direction, hoping to recognize a celebrity. Then he got a call and we had to park sideways across a street to stop traffic and help the firemen who were putting out the flames in a house. I was a prisoner for an hour and forty-five minutes in that car, listening to the idiot moaning on about Annie.

He pulled up a chair in front of me, took a sip, and stared into my eyes, nodding his head. I felt it coming . . .

"I loved that girl. A lot more than the rest of them. I'm over it now, I'm not hung up on her anymore, but when she left I had a hell of a time. I used to cry like a baby every night. I would have torn down the house if I'd had the strength, but I was completely wiped out. I was tired like I've never been in my whole life . . ."

"If I knew my licence number by heart, I suppose that would help things."

"I was hoping everything would work out, maybe she'd forgive me for having thrown her out, because I loved her so much it made me sick. Just walking by a restaurant where we used to go, just seeing a movie we'd seen together — it drove me crazy. Good thing I got over it. These days I'm all right, I'm out of the woods . . ."

"If you let me make a call, I think I could get ahold of someone who'd be able to give me my number. The old man I work with stayed back at the house to get it ready for the party after the fashion show, and —"

"Weeks went by. I had to get used to the fact that I'd never see her again. I'd never hold her in my arms again. I'd never see her naked, stretched out on the bed when I came into the room. I'd never get on top of her again, wanting to kill her because that was the only way to have her all to myself . . ."

"Yeah, that's great, but, like I was saying, if I could make a call, I'm sure we could clean this mess up in record time."

"What are you talking about?" he demanded, emerging

from his private fantasy, "do you know her number? Could you put in a good word for me?"

"No. But someone could get my licence from the truck and I could give you the number."

"Oh . . . that," he sighed, dropping into an abyss of despair at one hundred kilometres an hour. "Okay, come on, we'll find a phone."

We went down a long corridor, then through a big room. The cops who went by stopped, gave me a hateful look, or brushed their belts with their fingertips to make sure their guns were still there.

"Good thing," he went on, "that I've got her out of my mind. Forgotten! Wiped clean! I never think of her, she's really gone for good. But you know her, so you know what it's like: it's not easy forgetting a girl like her."

I dialled the number, praying to God to leave me half a chance. At least the line wasn't busy; so far, so good. It rang. And rang. And rang. Shit, was it ringing! What the hell are you up to, Granddad? Get off Azalée, pull on your undies, and answer the goddamn phone!

After a while, the cop pulled the receiver out of my grip.

"Doesn't look like anyone's home," he said with a smile.

I felt like bawling, getting down on my knees, and promising him whatever he wanted as long as he set me free. I pictured myself rotting away in a cell choked with cobwebs, and this madman still going on about Annie.

"You can't keep me here all night just because I forgot my licence in the glove compartment of my truck! I've got other things to do!"

"Go ahead, tell me if I'm boring you. That's it, go ahead and yawn."

"That's not it. I love your company, but someone I know's giving birth and . . . anyway, by now, it's probably all over. Is it too much to ask to be by her side?"

"I should be able to let you go as soon as we get proof you have a licence, and that there are no outstanding charges against you."

"What charges? What are you talking about? I didn't do anything! I was driving to the hospital in somebody else's car and I didn't have my damn licence, just a piece of paper. Shit, are you going to send me to prison for that?"

I hadn't realized it, but I was shouting at him as if he were deaf, and all the cops had turned around to look. A shiver ran down my spine. A big guy was striding up to me. He moved slowly, with the self-confidence of a man who's been in the business for a long time. He was grey around the temples, and I didn't know if it was that or his blue eyes, but I got the feeling that here was a guy with something between his ears.

"What's going on?"

"Speeding, Chief. And he didn't have his licence."

"I was going to the hospital, sir, a friend of mine is having her baby right now. She left with another policeman, and I had to drive her car."

"I see."

He looked the lovesick cop in the eye; the guy had a desperate look. Then he put his hand on the guy's shoulder.

"I'll take care of it now. You can go back to work."

The first cop turned away, and every step he took removed a little more weight from my shoulders. My saviour took out a pack of smokes and offered me one. I took it. I was in no position to refuse anything. He swept the lighter flame under my nose. I inhaled and kept an eye on the other guys who'd come closer to hear our conversation.

"Tell me, young man, I'd like to ask you a question."

"Go ahead."

"Have I ever told you about Annie?"

Naturally, those bums all burst out laughing.

The older cop put his arm on my shoulder and steered me towards the door.

"Thanks for your patience. And don't forget your licence next time you go for a drive."

"What does that mean?"

"It means you can leave. I think you've been punished enough."

Since this cop was a smart guy, I decided to keep my cool.

"And ease up on the gas pedal. Next time you might not be so lucky."

"Thanks," I said and offered my hand.

He surrounded it with his and began grinding my bones to dust. I skittered towards the exit with a dozen mocking smiles following my progress.

As I checked to see whether I had enough money to take a taxi to the Mustang, I thought of that love-crazed cop. I really messed up his week — he's going to head for the bottom and never come up. That didn't worry me. He'd get into his cruiser and start driving until it stuck in his craw like a scream. Then he'd take it out on some poor guy half his size, at the end of a dead-end alley or in a cell.

"Fuck off and die, shitface!"

•••

The woman at the desk directed me to the sixth floor. I ran to the elevator. The door opened as I got to it, and I jumped inside and pushed the button. The door snapped shut. Sometimes life is easy.

I stepped out, thirty metres from the waiting room. I saw Pierrot and the specialist through the glass doors. He turned to Annie, then collapsed in her arms. Fused together, they stood motionless, then Pierrot's head dropped onto Annie's shoulder. I kept walking, even if I was uncomfortable at the thought of disturbing them, and rushing things, shattering the crystal moment that united them. I wanted to stop but I couldn't. Couldn't slow down or turn back. I wanted to take off in the opposite direction, shoot off like a deer that's caught the scent of its own death, but I kept moving towards them.

Pierrot raised his head to catch his breath. I saw his eyes reddened by tears. He saw me, too, but had no reaction, except to look at the floor. Annie held him tighter. She was crying, too, I could see by the spasms that shook her back and made her shoulders shudder.

By the time I put my hand on the glass door, the first tear was rolling down my cheek. Pierrot lifted his eyes towards mine and I understood that things had gone terribly wrong. I took both of them in my arms and buried my hand in Pierrot's hair. We stood there for what seemed like forever, falling endlessly into darkness.

"Oh, Julien," Pierrot moaned, "Julien, oh, shit . . ."

Desperately, I grasped for the kind of strength that would help me fight this lousy war.

22

When the obstetrician came to talk to us and tell us what had happened, Pierrot was already like a desert, his eyes arid as he listened to the woman and acquiesced to everything she said, like a novice before the apparition of the Virgin. I kept my hand on his shoulder, figuring it couldn't hurt.

Listening to the terms she used, I couldn't tell whether she was talking about Sonia or the space shuttle. I suppose that's how they avoid getting completely depressed. You can't watch a twenty-six-year-old woman die before your eyes without asking a few questions about life. Questions you can't answer without turning to the rope, the gun, or the razor blade.

Annie sat down and looked at us through two strands of hair. I slid my hand onto her thigh, hoping to reassure her. The pain was twice as bad for her, the combination of Pierrot's tragedy and the thought that she'd have her feet in the same stirrups in four weeks. I felt like it was raining bombs, and that my job was to catch them all before they hit the ground. That didn't leave much time to look after my own mourning.

I didn't retain much of what the doctor said, only that it was a mindless accident, a combination of uncontrollable factors made worse by incredible bad luck. When the membranes broke, the cord got swept along in the uterus, carried by the movement of the waters. If the baby had been in the normal position, it probably would not have happened. But since it was feet-first, the cord had just enough space to slip through. By the time Sonia got to the hospital, fetal distress was already quite noticeable. The baby died a few minutes later. But that wasn't enough; Sonia had to scatter any remains of normalcy. She hit on the idea of an amniotic embolism. It was a great find. Everyone was bowled over. If you ask me, she preferred death to giving birth to a corpse.

After the conversation, Pierrot insisted on seeing her. The obstetrician seemed to think that wasn't necessarily such a good idea, but he yelled so loud that she immediately showed him the way in. I offered to go with him, but he wouldn't have it. I was relieved, actually. A nurse led him down the hall, then stopped in front of a door and spoke briefly to him. Pierrot nodded, she opened the door, he went into the room, and the nurse stayed outside as if nothing was the matter, as if she were waiting to use the toilet.

Another nurse came in, and the obstetrician asked her to give Annie something. Excellent idea, I thought. Both of them headed for another room, arms around each other's waist, like old friends. To glance at the people going about their business here, you wouldn't have thought that the roof had just caved in. But when you looked in their eyes, you could see it was so.

I got the feeling the obstetrician wanted to speak to me, but she seemed to be having trouble doing it. She sat down at her desk, and I saw she was more shaken than I'd thought. This was the first time I'd witnessed any sign of weakness from the woman. We'd known each other for a few months, since she was looking after Annie, too.

"Go ahead," I said. "I'm ready for anything."

She crossed her legs and took a deep breath.

"I'm telling you because I believe you're in the best position to understand what happened."

Sure — I was totally delighted with my position. I decided not to knock her teeth out; I let her talk.

"If you think this can help your friend, then tell him. On the other hand, if you think it's better to keep it a secret, do so. But don't say anything to Annie, at least not before the end of her pregnancy."

I wondered what she was going to spring on me now. I really was ready for anything. She could have told me, with one glance, that I was rotten with cancer and I would have believed her. Anything was possible on this planet, gone were the times when we could walk down the street, minding our own business like innocent fools. We had to keep our eyes peeled. At any moment, anything could happen to us. That truth had been proved once and for all and I didn't consider myself lucky enough to go on doubting it.

"The fact that the waters were greenish was a sign that the fetus was in difficulty. A substance we call meconium gives them that colour. The child evacuates it, but only after birth. When it's present before then, either the term has been exceeded or something has gone amiss."

"I imagine that something must have gone amiss. Otherwise, we'd all be wearing smiles, right?"

"The presence of meconium in the amniotic fluid probably precipitated the effects of the embolism."

I figured all that shit running through your veins wasn't there to help. But face it, life has a certain irony to it. The liquid that protects the fetus for nine months turns around and kills the mother at birth. What a stroke of genius!

The doctor kept her gaze trained on me a few more seconds, probably wondering whether she should go on, then she decided. She described the child to me and I understood why she didn't want me to talk it over with Annie.

When Pierrot emerged from the room, he had recovered some of his serenity. I asked no questions. He signed the papers, I took him by the shoulder, and we walked slowly towards the elevator. Annie followed us, holding a little bottle of pills against her stomach. The nurse went out of her way to convince her not to worry, Sonia's case was really extraordinary, she shouldn't be afraid of the same thing happening to her. Besides, her pregnancy was coming along normally, everybody agreed with that diagnosis. I felt like thanking God, but when I thought about Him, a taste of vomit popped up in my mouth.

The hospital evacuated us like a gang of stillborns a little after two in the morning. The parking lot was empty, the show was over, the audience had all gone home, there were only three bad actors left, with no stage direction and no script. We'd been in a state of shock for so long we began wondering whether it wasn't our normal condition.

For a time there, I thought we might be like that forever, with hearts panicking over everything and fog in our eyes. A kind of lethargy, a half-coma, overtook us, as if our unconscious had found a way to keep from soaking up too much of the present and erase those memories as quickly as possible. Three unruly hairs on life's bald head — that's what we were. I sat my butt down on the Mustang's bumper, gazed up at the sky, and caught my breath. I thought I saw a star giving me a nasty wink.

Later, at Pierrot's place, I tried to tell him my little secret. I didn't know if it was the right thing to do. I didn't have the strength to ask myself that question, but I just couldn't keep that putrid gob of spittle in my mouth anymore. But since Annie was always around, I had no choice but to chew over my poison.

We both smoked an industrial quantity of hash, while Annie took another pill from the bottle the nurse gave her. We slowly went crazy, lying on the living room floor. Annie cried silently. From time to time I looked over to see whether she had fallen asleep. No dice. She kept at it slowly but surely. She cried for Sonia and Pierrot, but I got the feeling she was crying for herself, too, for the vulnerability and powerlessness of the thing she carried inside her, that minuscule collection of cells that slaved away to become a healthy little body.

Pierrot still hadn't recovered the faculty of speech. When I muttered, "It's unreal," he simply nodded his head. As if he had decided he was better off agreeing than fighting or looking for answers to stupid questions. By being so accepting, he spared himself a lot of trouble and avoided a lot of painful subjects. But it was more than resignation; there was pure exhaustion, too. As if he were tired from a long trip. A round-trip ticket to Paradise and Hell — that kind of fatigue.

With all the beer we'd drunk besides the hash, Pierrot and I soon sank into a false sense of well-being, a sort of calmness, but only on the outside. But that was better than nothing.

Annie volunteered to announce the catastrophe to the old man and Azalée, who must have been waiting for us for a while now. She went towards the kitchen. I stayed with Pierrot; even if I couldn't steer him clear of the reef, this was no time to abandon the ship. Annie couldn't remember the number, and I had to shout it to her from the living room, as if it were the winning combination in some kind of funereal lottery.

She kept Granddad on the phone for a good twenty minutes. She told the whole story, down to the slightest detail, and from the speed at which she talked, I imagined that the old man must have been begging her to slow down.

Once that nasty bit of business was over, Annie came and buried her face between my shoulder and my neck. A tear or two slid under my T-shirt. I walked her to the bedroom, tucked her in, and bestowed a series of little kisses all over her, ending with her belly. She raised a pair of red eyes in my direction.

"It'll be okay," I whispered to her, trying to make myself believe that a curse like that couldn't happen twice in the same year.

I hung out with Pierrot a little more, in case a sudden need to scream came over him. I glanced in his direction once in a while to make sure his heart hadn't stopped, and every time I did, I was sure I saw Sonia sweeping through the kitchen door. I didn't mention it to Pierrot; it would have been ridiculous compared to what he must have been going through. I was the trailer; he, the double feature.

We still hadn't talked about the kid. We were so stoned, so disconnected from our bodies and the power of our feelings, that I decided to chance the question.

"How do you feel about the kid?"

"I don't know. It's like it's his fault."

I decided not to volunteer what the obstetrician had said. She hadn't gone into detail, besides telling me that with the malformations the kid suffered from, it was better for him not to have survived. A nightmare vision had taken root in my skull, a picture of a half-human, half-reptile creature, a sci-fi monster come from down below to feast on Sonia's guts.

I figured that knowing the kid was a monster wouldn't have helped Pierrot. Instead of trying to patch a kilometre-long wound with a Band-Aid, you might as well keep your big mouth shut.

23

"Listen, Pierrot," I said as I pulled out of a tight curve, "we talked it over and we both agree you should come and stay with us."

It had been a month since Sonia died, and I hadn't noticed the slightest improvement. He just couldn't get back on his feet again and grab a second wind.

"You can't stay in your apartment anymore," Annie added. "It's unhealthy."

"I know. But I can't live with you guys. We'll get in each other's way, it won't work out."

"It won't be forever. You know, just till the storm blows ovcr."

The worst part wasn't the days following death, the burial, and all that. The worst part was the period after the tragedy, when people went back to their daily lives, and meanwhile, there you were, with nobody and nothing to staunch the bleeding in your soul.

"What about the kid . . . ?"

"She'll sleep in our room. I'm sure you'll be able to help us out. With all the shit that's gone down lately, a little diaper won't be anything compared to that."

"Thanks a lot, I appreciate the offer, but I don't think so."

"Take your time, think about it, man."

The dashboard clock showed two thirty-four. Three consecutive numbers means I get to make a wish.

I stopped at the general store to buy some beer. The cool air of this first October day had driven the two old ladies deep into their store. I greeted them and walked to the fridge to take down two six-packs.

"How are things, young man?"

"Just fine."

"Mr. Landry told us about your friend's girlfriend. It's hard to imagine."

"It is."

"Is that him in the car with Annie?"

"Yes."

"Death certainly is something . . ."

Every time those two old ladies opened their mouths, the subject of death always came up. I suppose that once you've reached a certain age, it's the only way to get used to the fact that your day is coming soon. Death and you get to know each other, you woo each other, you kiss each other's fingertips, and when the big day comes, it's *yes*, for better or for worse.

"Are you going to be there tomorrow?" I asked, picking up my change.

"Oh, yes. We wouldn't miss it for all the tea in China."

The whole village knew; it was the event of the year. They wrote it up in the local paper in the "Social and Economic Development" column. Social, maybe. Economic? I didn't see it.

I got back into the car and handed the fruit of my purchases to Annie. She pulled a can off its plastic necklace and handed it to Pierrot. He opened it, took a big pull, then let loose with a tremendous belch. It was an expression of pain, like pissing in the face of destiny.

"I'll have a smoke about now," I announced, pulling out of the parking space. "Unfiltered, if you please."

Since Sonia's death, Pierrot had gone back to mistreating his body. When I wanted to prove to him that he wasn't alone, I did the same.

The Mustang rolled quietly through the village, but as soon as we hit the outskirts, I put my foot on the gas and ate up the centre line like a bulimic PacMan. All the windows were down and the raw wind came in and whipped our faces to its heart's content. It was the best way to prove we were still alive. That, and knowing that a momentary lack of vigilance could launch us into the great beyond. Annie slipped down into her seat, eyes closed, hands around her swollen belly. Pierrot watched the devastated, dried-out plots of earth flash by, like a mirror that projected his own image. The needle hit one hundred and fifty, and the Mustang gathered its strength in case we found an exit ramp that led out of hell.

We certainly had done our best since August. We hadn't left him alone a minute. Especially Annie, seeing as though she was in no mood to spend all day at the market, twiddling her thumbs. They took off together, they even rented a cottage on the coast for a week. They got it for a song, since the owner was a friend of the old man's. When they returned, they started cleaning up Sonia's things. Pierrot insisted that Annie take back all the clothes. She agreed, but wouldn't put on a single garment.

Every evening, the three of us got together to say what we'd done that day. Actually, the whole process bored us to tears, but we went on talking as a way to keep reality at bay. Once in a while, the old man and Azalée would join us, but there was no question of inviting Pierrot to the farm. Today was the first time.

I let up on the gas and slowed down just enough to keep us from rolling into the fields as I turned onto the little gravel road. Annie opened her eyes and made sure Pierrot was still there. She smiled at him, and he answered with a kind of absurd cackle.

"I hope I won't fuck up too bad here."

We stopped in front of the house. The old man was running the vacuum over the front steps. We got out of the car and walked right up to him before he realized we were there.

"There you are!" he exclaimed as he turned off the machine. "I wasn't expecting you so soon."

"It's three o'clock, Granddad, just like I told you."

"Three o'clock already? That can't be, I haven't even cleaned the oven."

Pierrot got the beer out of the Mustang and gave us each one. The four of us sat down on the steps and looked at our shoes. The old man was sweating. I offered to take over from him.

"That would be nice, Julien."

"You look pretty tired."

"I know I do."

"You have to take it easy, Granddad," Annie smiled. "You'll need all your strength for your wedding night. She won't take age as an excuse."

The usual rude comments followed. The old man looked at each one of us and smiled when it was appropriate. For a few seconds, we forgot our pain and all the things that make you want to blow this world sky-high. A good laugh lifts you above the little details, it gets you back to the essentials. Even Pierrot smiled.

Naturally, after a few seconds, the shadows returned. It wasn't easy coming back here. It affected us, too, but we couldn't crack up at every opportunity, otherwise, who would he cling to? He needed a life preserver with a certain amount of stability, a piece of rock, instead of quicksand. So we swallowed it back and, in the long run, that made us forget quicker. Cruel, but true. You can live with the dead as long as you recognize the line between the two. I could go on at some length about the phenomenon, take my word for it.

The hardest part for me was keeping the secret. Often I would watch Pierrot and try to imagine what would happen if I told him. Either it would provide him a way of accepting half the tragedy, or it would lead to complete catastrophe. One thing's for sure: you don't drop a bomb like that one without a mushroom cloud rising up on the horizon somewhere.

"Where's Azalée?" Annie asked.

"With her mother. She'll be here tomorrow, at eleven. I think it's ridiculous, but I'm willing to do it for her."

"It's her right," I told him.

We're always doing ridiculous things for women, putting up with their whims just to hold onto them a little bit longer. But why not? It's not a bad thing to know we're willing to turn ourselves inside out for the thing we desire.

Pierrot stuck another unfiltered cigarette in his mouth. On the screen inside his head, I knew he was watching another two or three reels of memories. No intermission, no popcorn, and the same damned unreal ending. But he had no choice; he had to revisit every place he'd been with her. It was like an allergy: you have to stuff your body full of it if you want to be able to face it in the future without your eyes going red. Call it desensitizing. It works in any number of fields.

He scratched a match and moved the flame towards his cigarette, eyes scanning the horizon line. He looked like a guy dying of thirst, who's been promised an oasis over the next dune in this eternal desert.

24

Annie was sleeping on her side. I ran my hand over her big belly and took advantage of her sleep to get close to her enormous breasts. The belly was always eager for caresses, but lately, the breasts had become off-limits. Then I pulled on my jeans and went outside for a breath of fresh air.

It was a Kodacolor day. Fantastic. The blues and greens were exploding, just like the weather girl predicted. I resolved to send her flowers. A sunbeam hit me full in the face and it was good. Invisible life, tiny particles that come sweeping down on you at top speed, thousands of minuscule fireflies that have flown from the sun like rockets and haven't slowed down since, haven't said, "Hey, why don't we stop for a beer?" No, they keep on running like crazy, without looking back to where they came from or wondering where they're going. They keep on coming, that's all there is. And here we are on our big rotten ball, wondering why we're born and why we have to die, and we can't even run from here to the next block without grabbing our guts with both hands.

I decided to drop in on Dalida. She watched me come in, hay hanging out of her mouth, as if she were saying to herself, "Well, it's about time. But where's the old man? Well, why not, it does a cow's pride good to take on a tender young thing every once in a while."

I sat down on the little stool and tapped her on the side. First you have to clean the udder, and be careful about it, because you never know when you're going to get an eyeful of cowtail when she tries to brush away a fly. Milking itself is no mystery. You put one hand at the base of the udder, you squeeze firmly, then pull down. I went to it: squeeze, pull, let up. Squeeze, pull, let up . . .

Someone opened the door and Dalida turned around. She obviously wondered who would dare interrupt us in the middle of our work. Pierrot was there. He looked like a guy who hadn't slept all night.

"Hi," I said, taking in the extent of the damage. "Did you sleep a little?"

"I couldn't stop thinking."

What can you say after that? *Don't worry, good buddy, another girl will come along.* No way, I'm sorry, you can't say anything to a guy who's been through the wringer of memory.

"I wasn't even thinking about Sonia. That's the worst part."

"Who were you thinking about?"

I should have guessed; he was talking about the kid. It should have been obvious. If not Sonia, it must have been the kid.

"I wasn't thinking about the kid, either," he informed me.

"I was thinking about the guy."

"What guy?" I asked with a frown. "Listen, Pierrot, stop talking in riddles if you want to make yourself understood."

"The guy who killed her," he declared, biting his lower lip.

If you ask me, that wasn't a very good sign. I'd suspected lately that it was bugging him. Now he'd finally made it his obsession.

"Listen to what I'm going to tell you, man. It wasn't some guy who killed her, the kid didn't kill her, it was just plain bad luck."

"If she hadn't gotten pregnant, Julien, she'd still be here today."

"If you want to extrapolate that far, let me take it one step further. If she hadn't met you, it wouldn't have happened either."

"Don't talk shit."

"You're the one talking shit, Pierrot. You're the one flipping out."

"I think I've got the right to."

"There's where you're wrong. You don't have any rights at all. Okay, you've got the right to spit on the whole world if you want to, but that's as far as it goes. You don't have the right to put the blame on anybody else. We're all on the same level, we're all here to fuck up each other's lives. Don't confuse a murderer and an instrument because they're not the same thing."

"You don't understand, Julien, you don't understand how bad it hurts. You don't understand, every minute of the day I just want to keel over dead, just like her. When you're hurting, you can lean your head on Annie, you can put your face between her breasts or between her legs. Life will console you. When I'm hurting, I've got nothing to turn to — just death."

I'd stopped squeezing, pulling, and letting up. My rhythm had gone off and Dalida was starting to get impatient. Pierrot leaned against the side of the stall, trying to hide his trembling chin. I was willing to say anything to bring him back to life, but I was starting to suffer from fatigue of the imagination.

"You know, Pierrot, I don't think Sonia would like to see you like this."

"That's bullshit and you know it!"

I did know it. But since I'd already played my best cards, I had to settle for whatever was in my hand.

"Sonia doesn't exist," he started up again. "Neither here, nor up above, nor down below. She doesn't exist and some asshole has to answer for that."

"What are you talking about?" I asked, pulling the metal bucket from under Dalida.

"I'm going to find him."

"Pierrot, you're out of your mind. How are you going to do that? You don't know anything about him, you have no clues, you don't know where to start."

"I have a phone number."

"A phone number? Where did you find that?"

"In Sonia's notebook. On the inside cover. It was written sideways, with the name André, and a number underneath it."

"What makes you think it's the number you're looking for?"

"It's not Sonia's writing."

"I see. You're going to dial the number, and ask for

André, then you'll say hello, excuse me for disturbing you, but I'd like to know if you slept with a certain girl the night of November 30 to December 1 of last year."

"Why not?"

"If Sonia hadn't wanted you to know, that means you shouldn't know. She took that secret with her, and there must be a reason for it."

"Then why did she leave the telephone number?"

"What proves it's his?"

"Nothing. I just get the feeling it's the kind of thing you scribble down before you slip away the morning after. Maybe it's not him. I can always go to the bar near her place. I'm sure that's where she met him."

The chances were good that she'd picked him up there. It wouldn't have been too difficult for her. Every time she went anywhere, a gang of guys was ready to lie down and act as her carpet.

"I'm going there and I'm going to question everybody until somebody breaks."

"Great! And when you know who it is, you're going to take his picture and decorate your room at the asylum with it?"

"No. I'm going to kill him."

You know what? I didn't think he was exaggerating.

"What are you talking about?"

"I'm telling you, Julien, I'm going to kill him. I'm going to kill him where he stands and no one can stop me. I'm going to kill him, I'm telling you, and that's the only thing that keeps me alive."

A few beads of sweat shone on his forehead and little red patches appeared around his mouth and nose. I could practically see his heart pounding beneath his T-shirt. I took his hand and made him sit down where I'd been.

"It's time to calm down, man."

He took a deep breath of air and closed his eyes. He was totally exhausted.

"I'm losing my mind, Julien. I really think I'm going crazy."

"It's normal, Pierrot, you're depressed. You're totally down — it's normal to go a little bit crazy. You'll come back to yourself, you'll get better one of these days."

I kept his hand in mine. When he started to cry, I felt like dying.

"You know what?" I said. "If you talked about it a little more, it might help you get out of it."

"It all seems so useless," he sniffed, "you wouldn't understand anyway."

"Let me tell you something: I felt the exact same thing. Sure, people can't understand everything, but talking helps. Remember, when you're fighting this kind of battle, you're not better off alone."

"I'm afraid you guys'll think I don't want to get out of it. I'm afraid you'll think I'm starting to go off the deep end."

"Don't worry, man, we'll never think that."

Dalida's tail swept through the air by his ear. The cow must have noticed something we couldn't see.

Pierrot shrugged his shoulders.

"I guess you're right, Julien."

"About what?"

"If it's just for a little while, if I help out with the kid, we won't really get on each other's nerves."

"No. Not really."

25

We'd just finished getting everything ready when the people started arriving. A few minutes later, there were twenty of us between the house and the barn. The two old ladies from the general store were among the first to come. They took up position right at the front. I asked them if everything was fine; it was. We'd made coffee, but they preferred to wait for something a little stronger.

A few minutes later, five farmers' trucks turned onto the dirt track and raised a great cloud of dust. Mrs. Fournier from the market got out first, scanning the horizon for a good match for her daughter. Then Charlotte made her appearance, as refreshing as a carpet of dew after a row of hot coals. The realization was stunning and immediate: I must have been completely disconnected not to love that girl when I had the chance.

They both came over to kiss me. When the mother placed

her dry lips against my cheek, for a second I was afraid she'd ask me if Annie really was the girl for me. But she settled for a sigh. Then I got a mouthful of Charlotte. I pressed my lips against her cheek and it felt wonderfully soft and warm. I would have gladly visited the other cheek but Annie's eyes were boring holes in the back of my neck. I wasn't about to risk decapitation.

Bill and Paule arrived. Bill got out of the car, arms loaded down with diapers, playpens, and pacifiers, while Paule held the object of all that attention firmly against her body. I swear, eight of us could have fallen upon her and we still wouldn't have managed to separate her from the little beast. It was Baby's first time out in the world and Paule wasn't about to share the glory. Naturally, Annie rushed right over to kiss her and try to get her hands on the kid. Not that she didn't have certain privileges in that department; after all, she'd helped the mother during labour when Bill's business had taken him out of town. For Annie, it was the perfect opportunity to get back into the obstetric mood and prove that sometimes things do turn out all right.

When Paule's labour began, we had all headed for the hospital, to the sinister sixth floor. Annie held her hand as I smoked a couple dozen cigarettes and chowed down on two or three fingernails. Paule went in at eight o'clock in the morning and by noon it was all over. Personally, every time a door opened, I nearly lost consciousness. Life had taught me one thing: the impossible does happen. The only rough spot was between Annie and the obstetrician. When the little head started showing, Annie dropped Paule's hand and begged the doctor to let her bring the baby out. Obviously, she refused, and Annie told her to screw off.

As soon as they got into the house, they laid the baby on the table and everyone held their noses with both hands as brave Bill changed her diaper. I stole a baleful glance at Annie's stomach and realized that, if I thought I'd been in deep shit before, it was nothing compared to what awaited me now.

Ten minutes later, strange music issued forth from the sky. The kind of music that four or five large Afro-American singers with caps and gym shoes make. Then the sky was made flesh in the figure of a battered orange Plymouth. A two-hundred-dollar car with a fifteen-hundred-dollar sound system in it. Three young black guys were in front; Azalée, her mother, and her sister were jammed in the back. They pulled their car to a stop a little bit off to the side. Azalée and her mother came up to us, while the other four calmly took up position on the hood of the wreck. I knew we weren't going to throw rocks at each other, but still, someone had to take the first step and establish contact between the two clans. Pierrot sacrificed himself once the newcomers fired up a joint.

In the end, the whole gang greeted each other, and gave their names and the benefit of their comments about the old man and Azalée, obviously neglecting to mention either age or colour. Brotherhood reigned. Who says that drugs are the work of the devil?

The hearse arrived next. Even if all the locals knew the priest and his brother were inside, and that the latter acted as both undertaker and caterer, a cold wind of fear swept across the farm. The embalmer was at the wheel, the priest practised his sermon in the death seat, and the cold cuts reposed in the back.

Being outsiders, Azalée and her mother were shaken by the strange sight. I thought I'd better reassure them. Annie had the same idea, and we joined up next to them as I slipped an arm around her waist.

"Don't worry, Azalée," Annie said. "It's just the wedding feast."

"It seems strange to me. For a while, I thought something had gone wrong."

"Not at all," I pointed out. "Actually, it's so you can get rid of the body after the wedding night."

"How is he?" she asked.

"Fine, fine," I answered, idly watching three kids who were trying to trample a hen. Last night, when I got here, I thought he'd looked pretty tired. He still hadn't recovered today. "I'll go look for him."

"Come with me, Azalée," Annie ordered, taking her by the arm. "I'll help you put on your dress."

The house was deserted. After all the uproar outside, the silence was a blessing. Suddenly life seemed so simple that an inane smile spread across my face. I went through the kitchen and the living room, feeling as light as the strings of a harp.

"You've got half an hour," I yelled as I threw open the bedroom door.

The old man was sitting on the edge of the bed, his face buried in his hands. My simple-minded happiness was instantaneously crushed.

"What's wrong?"

He didn't move. That had me worried. I knew we were up against something solid, but I wasn't about to give in.

"What's the matter, Granddad?"

"We're calling it off," he whimpered.

"What are you talking about? What's going on?"

"I can't do it, Julien. I can't do that to her," he said, running his hand through his white mane.

"Do what to her? Stop talking crap and explain yourself."

"She won't even be forty when I die."

"Great! It won't be too late for her to start a new life."

"I'm cancelling it. I can't do it."

"Sorry, old man, you can't. Everyone's here: the priest, the undertaker, everybody."

"You don't understand, Julien, I can't do it."

"Well, you should have thought about that earlier. I bought you a wedding present, and I don't want to end up with a pair of extra-large edible underpants."

"I don't want her to have to take care of me when I'm too old to get around."

"Don't worry, it won't happen."

"How can you be so sure?"

"As soon as you can't get it up anymore, she'll head for the hills."

"You can bullshit all you want, but I know what it's like to look after an old person. I took care of my wife until I didn't have an ounce of strength left."

Though we'd hardly ever talked about it, I knew those hadn't been the most pleasurable days of his life. When you watch a woman coming apart at the seams right before your eyes, until you can't let her out of your sight, even long enough to go to the can, it can't be much fun.

"By the time she died," he said in a broken voice, "I'd long been dead."

"I believe you. Only thing is, right now, you're very

much alive, and you'd better seize the day, because there's a whole line of old codgers like you just waiting for a pretty young thing to look in their direction."

He rubbed his eyes for a few seconds, then looked right into mine.

"Okay. But promise me one thing."

"Anything you like."

"Julien, I'm serious, I want you to promise me. You'll see, it's no joke. If you ever think that I'm a burden for her, I want you to convince her to leave me."

"Come on, she'd never do that."

"If she says no, if pity is the only thing keeping her with me, if I can't get around, or if I've lost my mind, I want you to kill me."

"Do you mind repeating that?"

"I want you to kill me."

Murder seems to be going around these days.

"Come on, Granddad, you've completely lost it. You know I couldn't do something like that."

"That's what people say. But when the time is right, sometimes we find the courage we need to act."

"What are you talking about?"

He looked at me silently with his old drunkard's eyes, two old eyes overflowing with water and regret, and suddenly I understood what he meant. He was talking about his wife.

"I see," I whistled as I sank down next to him.

He lifted one hand and brought it down heavily on my thigh.

"If ever a day comes when I ask you to do it, I want to make sure you won't refuse. If I do the asking, it's not a crime, understand?"

I almost told him to stop thinking about that stuff, but that was the reality of old folks' lives. Who was I to advise him with the accumulated wisdom of my twenty-seven years? "Come on, Granddad, what are you going on about? You ain't dead yet! That's no way to look at life!" I knew that every morning, when he got out of bed, he felt just a little heavier, a little more fragile, a little closer to death.

"Okay, I promise, I'll keep it in mind. But now, trust me, let life spoil you a little, don't miss out on the good years you have left."

Years I could actually count.

"Besides, Granddad, we've got to get going. It's your wedding, damnit, not your funeral. Smile! *Smile!*"

I wanted this day to be a total success, even if it poured, hailed, or rained shit. I galloped into the kitchen, howling like crazy. Through the window, I spied the people awaiting us: Pierrot, eyes squinting, nodding at everything Azalée's sister was telling him; Annie, patting her stomach as she cast a tender eye on the three little brats plucking the chicken; Bill, solving square roots as he rubbed his ear lobe; Paule, rubbing her lips against her daughter's forehead and jabbing her elbow into Bill's ribs simultaneously; Azalée's mother, harassing her rosary as she stared suspiciously at the hearse; and everyone else whom I knew, more or less, whose destiny I controlled over the next few seconds. Suddenly I felt like drawing out the moment. I grabbed the bottle of Scotch and came back with another whoop and holler.

"What are you up to now?" he asked.

"Get up, old man, we're going to suck back a few before we head out. Then we'll show those numb-nuts a thing or two."

We drank like a couple of pigs, passing the bottle back and forth like it was holy communion. The stuff hit our bellies like concentrated sunshine. I figured my mind would fog over completely, but just the opposite happened. I felt so lucid all of a sudden that I wondered if I hadn't been comatose all this time. Annie came into the room a few millilitres later to tell us to get our asses in gear. I looked her in the eye and she seemed so beautiful to me that I ripped the bottle out of the old man's grip, toasted her, and swallowed down the last pull.

In the kitchen, we righted Granddad's bow tie and kissed him on both cheeks.

"It's your move, old man."

He aimed his body at the door and headed for it. Annie made a move to follow but I held her back by one overall strap. I took her head between my hands and put my lips on hers. She stuck her tongue into my mouth with such ferocity that, if it weren't for that belly of hers that was about to explode at any minute, we would have set the furniture flying in the kitchen. I slipped my hand down the front of her shirt anyway. One big breast came to rest in my palm and its nipple, as hard as concrete, forced apart my index and middle finger. The main thing wasn't necessarily to fuck ourselves to death — even if I feared my shorts would never go back to normal after the erection they'd had to hold in — but for her to know that, even with her beach-ball shape, she was still the most beautiful woman around.

We stumbled into the blinding light of this golden morning as our pupils shrank at the speed of sound. The few conversations still going on stilled to a murmur, then faded. The guests were there and the priest was waiting for our appearance. The old man was hanging out by the door; Annie slipped her arm under his and they stepped up to the padre.

Red-faced, unsteady on my feet, I found Azalée behind the barn. She was so beautiful I couldn't help rushing over to her and showering her with compliments.

"Everything all right?" I asked her once I'd finished.

"Sure. What about you?"

"Don't you worry about me, Azalée. Standing up for the next thirty minutes will be nothing compared to keeping my head above water for the last twenty-seven years."

We took a deep breath and left our quarters. The reaction was immediate; the audience was spellbound. A bird even crashed into a tree because it couldn't keep its eyes off her. We moved down the main aisle formed by the chairs. Granddad was already mopping his brow, even though we'd hardly travelled half the distance. I took back my arm and Azalée stepped up to him as I stopped at Annie's side.

The priest cleared his throat, then started in on his delivery. The words he spoke touched me as if they were meant for Annie and me. Ironic, wasn't it? Once upon a time I thought I would emerge victorious from that battle. Well, Annie's belly was proof that she had definitely won the war.

"Azalée Toussaint, do you take . . ."

Granddad, Pierrot, and I had watched the women streak by like falling stars in the night, and we couldn't say a word or lift a finger. They had invaded our lives and turned everything upside down with their nuclear hormones and their atomic uteruses.

"Pierre-Paul Landry, do you take . . ."

What about the little girl on the way? Would she imitate

her mother and annihilate her doddering father? Would I feel the same sting when I laid my cheek against her chest? Would it tear me up inside the same way? What would my rights be when she decided it was time to knock down the walls and flatten the fences? None at all?

"In that case, I declare you husband and wife. You may kiss the bride."

The blushing bride and groom joined their lips timidly, but the whole thing soon degenerated into a tartar-removing session. The old man knew what he was getting into, seeing that it was his second suicide.

I cast my eyes upon Annie. She stood silent, motionless, in the midst of the shouting, noisy crowd. I could tell from the way she looked at me that she was willing to do anything to carve out a little niche for us on this rotten planet. I knew she really loved me.

I moved towards her and her belly and breasts came to rest against me. My hands travelled over her butt and my nose burrowed into her sweet-smelling neck. It's true, I want the same thing, Annie. More than anything else in the world, even if it's the end of me, even if I lose myself in you, I want it, too. I want that little creature that'll soon see the light of day, I want her to spin me impossible stories, I want her to tear apart my life like the sound of squeaking chalk in a silent cathedral. I want us to grow old together under this damn sky of blue. I want to live like crazy, at two hundred kilometres an hour, I want to devour life like it was going out of style. I want to swallow time, devour the great beach of time, swallow it down whole, standing solid, jaws open wide, beneath the great hourglass of eternity.